SONAR™ 5

OVERDRIVE!

EXPERT QUICK TIPS

James Christensen

THOMSON

COURSE TECHNOLOGY

Professional ■ Technical ■ Reference

SONAR™ 5
OVERDRIVE!
EXPERT QUICK TIPS

Publisher and General Manager, Thomson Course Technology PTR: Stacy L. Hiquet

Associate Director of Marketing: Sarah O'Donnell

Manager of Editorial Services: Heather Talbot

Marketing Manager: Mark Hughes

Senior Acquisitions Editor: Todd Jensen

Marketing Coordinator: Jordan Casey

Developmental Editor: Orren Merton

Project Editor: Jenny Davidson

Technical Reviewer: Scott Stepenuck

PTR Editorial Services Coordinator: Elizabeth Furbish

Copyeditor: Kezia Endsley

Interior Layout Tech: Shawn Morningstar

Cover Designer: Mike Tanamachi and Nancy Goulet

Indexer: Sherry Massey

SONAR is a trademark of Twelve Tone Systems, Inc.

All other trademarks are the property of their respective owners.

Important: Thomson Course Technology PTR cannot provide software support. Please contact the appropriate software manufacturer's technical support line or Web site for assistance.

Thomson Course Technology PTR and the author have attempted throughout this book to distinguish proprietary trademarks from descriptive terms by following the capitalization style used by the manufacturer.

Information contained in this book has been obtained by Thomson Course Technology PTR from sources believed to be reliable. However, because of the possibility of human or mechanical error by our sources, Thomson Course Technology PTR, or others, the Publisher does not guarantee the accuracy, adequacy, or completeness of any information and is not responsible for any errors or omissions or the results obtained from use of such information. Readers should be particularly aware of the fact that the Internet is an ever-changing entity. Some facts may have changed since this book went to press.

Educational facilities, companies, and organizations interested in multiple copies or licensing of this book should contact the publisher for quantity discount information. Training manuals, CD-ROMs, and portions of this book are also available individually or can be tailored for specific needs.

The Thomson Course Technology PTR logo and related trade dress are trademarks of Thomson Course Technology and may not be used without written permission.

THOMSON

COURSE TECHNOLOGY

Professional ■ Technical ■ Reference

ISBN: 1-59200-627-2

Library of Congress Catalog Card Number: 2004114492

Printed in the United States of America

06 07 08 09 10 PH 10 9 8 7 6 5 4 3 2 1

Thomson Course Technology PTR, a division of Thomson Course Technology 25 Thomson Place Boston, MA 02210

http://www.courseptr.com

For Richard, Ella, Karen, and Jen.
I love you with all my heart.

Acknowledgments

This book would not be possible without the incredible people at Cakewalk, many of whom are my friends.

A very special thanks to Jesse Recinos, who provided ideas and text.

Much thanks to Bill Jackson for his many tips and infectious enthusiasm and to Aurelio Ramos for letting me steal some of his copious gray matter.

Thanks to Bob Damiano, Bob Currie, Jamie O'Connell, Alex Westner, John McCarty, Melissa Misicka, Clyde Cortright, Stephan Cocron, Jeremy Parker, Morten Saether, and to all the SONAR users I've been in contact with over the years.

A shout out to Greg Hendershott for starting Cakewalk.

About the Author

James Christensen is both a songwriter and a technical writer, working most recently in that capacity as the Principal Technical Writer at Cakewalk for nearly 7 years. He has written dozens of manuals, honing his technical chops by documenting SONAR during the day and recording and editing with it at night. Now a freelance writer and full-time musician, James Christensen is currently signed with Rolling Tongue Records and released his second album *Bull Rush* in the fall of 2005.

TABLE OF ♭ Contents

} Introduction

If you have spent any time recording music on a PC, chances are you have used or know someone who has used SONAR. Often considered the ideal solution for hobbyists and semi-professionals, SONAR is rarely given credit for being the full-featured, powerful program that it is. That thinking is changing, however, as more and more producers and engineers working with major artists now use SONAR as the heart of their studio setup. Make no mistake, SONAR is no toy; other digital audio products have nothing on SONAR, but it is also a first-rate MIDI sequencer.

I spent the better part of the last decade writing the manuals for SONAR and its predecessor, Pro Audio. And I also used them, at home, and in the studio. I learned two very important things during that time: The people at Cakewalk work every day to make their software the best it can be, and SONAR is the most feature-rich program I have ever used. I never stopped finding new things about SONAR, and with new features coming out every year, the folks at Cakewalk never rest. It's no wonder that they have a large, loyal following of customers who have been using SONAR since it was called Pro Audio (and some who have been around since it was called simply "Cakewalk"). They know what they are getting: quality and functionality. They know it because they have experienced it over the years.

This book is for you if you are looking to get faster at the things you already know how to do, want to learn ways around common pitfalls, and want to save yourself headaches. Each of the eight chapters covers one or more aspects of SONAR. There is something for everyone, from setting up, to sharing your files with others, to recording, to editing, to creating your final mastered tracks. It can be a reference you can turn to when you are trying to solve a problem, or a source for new ideas. Each tip is short and to the point, with numbered steps where appropriate, so you can spend less time in the book and more time creating music and sound.

Many of the tips in this book come from my own experiences working with SONAR. I'm a believer in SONAR, not only because of my time working there, but also because I've been recording my own material for years. I've never had a need for another sequencer, audio editor, or DXi host. SONAR has been my tool of choice. Other tips in this book come from the programmers, technical support engineers, quality assurance engineers, and product managers who work or have worked on SONAR. I've also spoken with other SONAR users who are quick to share the wealth of their knowledge.

I hope you find this book helpful and that it brings you closer to achieving your musical goals.

James Christensen

1 } Setup

Before you invest a lot of time and effort recording, it's a good idea to make sure your computer, operating system, and SONAR are all configured for the best performance possible. This can save you innumerable headaches down the road.

Configuring Your Hard Drive for Maximum Track Count

Although hard drives are becoming faster and cheaper, to attain near-limitless track counts or to work with video, using multiple hard drives is a necessity. Multiple hard drive configurations can provide more storage, more throughput, and a measure of security for your valuable data. Although SCSI drives have long been the darling of the A/V community, current technology has elevated ATA drives to a similar level of performance at a fraction of the cost. Because almost all new computers include at least one ATA hard drive, this tip will focus on how to extend and optimize these drives.

Note that ATA drives currently come in two varieties: IDE drives (Parallel ATA) or SATA (Serial ATA). This refers to how the drives interface with the motherboard and each other; SATA is the newer standard and offers a slightly increased theoretical bandwidth and easier setup. You can easily identify which type you have by the cables. Parallel ATA drives use wide ribbon cables (though round cables are now popular) while Serial ATA uses thin (1/4" wide) cables. Often a manufacturer will make the same drive available in both formats so the specifications of the drives are often the same.

Dedicated Audio Drive

The most common scenario uses a single additional drive exclusively to write and read audio data. The drive should be at least 7200 RPM and use ATA100 or SATA. (While there are now 10,000 RPM drives, these tend to generate quite a bit more noise in return for minimal performance increases during sustained transfer.) As important as adequate drive speed is, the bandwidth of the bus that the drives are connected to can also be a limiting factor. Therefore, it is recommended that you connect your dedicated drive to a different bus than the main boot drive. Systems using PATA will use busses labeled Primary and Secondary and those with SATA number them as 0/1/2/3 etc. This dedicated drive should preferably not share with any other drives. If the drive must share a cable and/or bus, use a CD-ROM or other drive not used constantly by Windows.

Be aware that you will not achieve any of these benefits by merely partitioning a drive. In fact, when you partition a drive, subsequent partitions are located closer to the center of the hard drive platter meaning potentially slower speeds. If you are partitioning the new drive, make sure that the first partition is reserved for audio.

After configuring and setting up your drives in Windows, make sure that SONAR is utilizing the correct drive by changing the default audio directory under Options > Global > Audio Data (see Figure 1.1). Note that when you are using per-project audio, the audio folder is stored on the same drive as the project file.

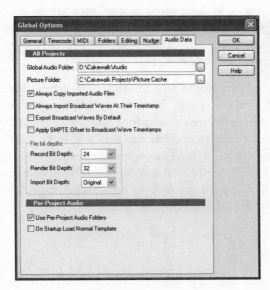

Figure 1.1

The Audio Data tab in the Global Options dialog.

RAID Arrays

A slightly more advanced option uses two or more dedicated drives to create a RAID (Redundant Array of Inexpensive Disks) array (even the name is redundant). By using a RAID controller card, either built into the motherboard or on the PCI bus, multiple drives can be configured so that the operating system sees them as one drive.

In a RAID 0 setup the drives are "striped," giving the benefit of double the storage capacity and also twice the theoretical transfer rate. This will be of primary interest to those working with very high resolution audio or video files. Though this is technically a RAID array, be aware that there is actually no redundancy. In fact, the chance of failure is twice as high than with one single drive because failure of one drive ruins all your data. When using this system, you should always back up projects or bundle files to a separate drive.

Another form of RAID is RAID 1, also known as "mirroring." This is true redundancy because data is written simultaneously to two or more drives. Read speeds benefit slightly in that the computer can read from both drives at the same time. Failure of either drive is not fatal, because the information is mirrored on the other drive. Although this offers maximum safety, there is little in the way of performance enhancements and you still have the capacity of only one drive. These may be relatively minor concerns compared to the integrity of your files however.

RAID 3 and RAID 5 are the most efficient forms of RAID as they combine the benefits of RAID 0 and RAID 1. Data is striped across multiple drives and each drive also keeps a record of what is stored on every other drive, which means that the failure of one single drive is not fatal; in fact, it can even be swapped out. The disadvantages of this system are the number of drives necessary to make this system worthwhile and the cost that goes along with that. Also, unlike RAID 0 and RAID 1, which are supported by the built-in controllers on most motherboards, RAID 3 and RAID 5 will mostly like require a specialized controller card, further adding to the cost. If you are working with a large number of A/V files or you run a separate server to share files with multiple computers on your network, this may be a solution to consider.

Modifying the Processor Scheduling Option for Use with ASIO

When using ASIO (Asynchronous Streaming Input Output) drivers with most professional audio interfaces, you can experience significant increases in performance by adjusting the priority of background of processes in Windows. The logic is that many of the associated services for the interface run as background tasks, thus when they are given priority, you can utilize lower latency settings without static, "crackling," or other audio anomalies. To set the Processor Scheduling to give priority to Background Services, do the following:

1. Choose Start > Settings > Control Panel.
2. In the Control Panel, double-click on System.
3. The System Properties dialog box appears (see Figure 1.2).

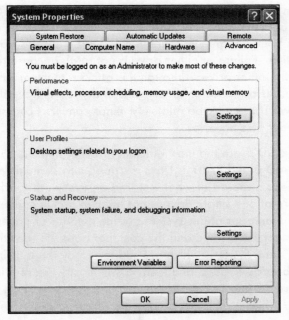

Figure 1.2

The System Properties dialog box.

4. Click the Advanced tab.
5. In the Advanced tab, click the Settings button in the Performance section.
6. In the Performance Options dialog box, click the Advanced tab.
7. Set the Processor Scheduling to give priority to Background Services (see Figure 1.3).

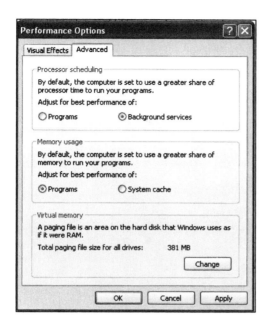

Figure 1.3
The Advanced tab of the
Performance Options dialog box.

Using Auto Save to Back Up as You Work

Imagine this—you are really getting into editing, when your computer crashes. If you have Auto Save enabled, you lost little or nothing. The Auto Save feature gives you a flexible tool for preserving your work even when you are too engrossed to click the Save button from time to time.

Use this procedure for setting up Auto Save in SONAR:

1. Choose Options > Global from the SONAR menu.
2. In the Global Options dialog box, click the General tab (see Figure 1.4).
3. Enter a value in either the Minutes or Changes field.

If you need your auto-saved project, choose File > Open and select the file appended with the words *Auto-Save Copy of.*

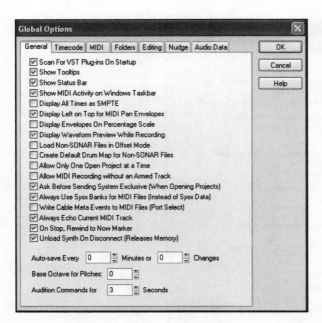

Figure 1.4
Global Options dialog box.

Adjusting XP System Options for Maximum Performance

There are options in Windows XP that, when configured correctly, can give you more performance enhancements. Settings in your Registry, along with Virtual Memory and other system options, are covered in the following two tips.

Editing System Variables and Registry Settings

By default, XP is set up to dazzle users with visual effects, automate day-to-day tasks, and provide a measure of security and backup. This does not even take into account all of the third-party software that is installed on most machines. For serious audio recording and mixing use, these tasks can get in the way.

Most of these tasks are loaded when the computer first boots up, but the Startup Menu folder is rarely used these days. Windows XP provides a tool that allows you to access all of the services and applications called on startup, called the System Configuration Utility.

1. Go to Start > Run. Type **MSCONFIG** and press Enter.

2. In the General tab, choose Selective Startup (see Figure 1.5).

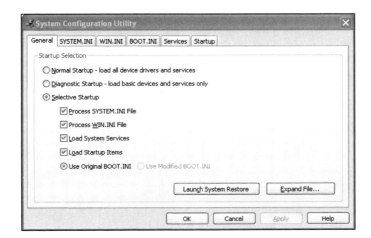

Figure 1.5

XP System
Configuration Utility
dialog box—
General tab.

3. Click on the Services tab. Here you will see many services that you might
   not recognize. Check Hide All Microsoft Services. Now you can freely
   uncheck items without fear of causing permanent damage. Looking in the
   Manufacturer column should give you an idea of which services do what
   (see Figure 1.6).

4. Now go to the Startup tab and continue to uncheck items. You might
   want to look at the Command or Location columns to get an idea of what
   the various tasks do. Occasionally, your sound card launches services
   such as its mixer utility at startup; you should leave settings like these as is.
   Other tasks include video card utilities, backup and anti-virus programs,
   and common applications like Winamp, MSN Messenger, and QuickTime.

5. After you've made these changes, simply click OK and restart your machine.

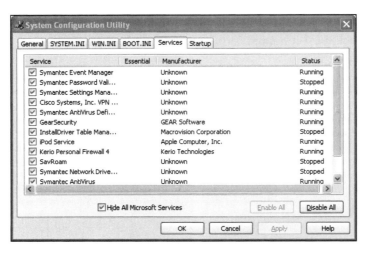

Figure 1.6

XP System
Configuration dialog
box—Services tab.

Configuring the Size and Location of Your Paging File

Having a lot of RAM is great—and necessary—when running SONAR. But you can get even more out of your machine if you take the time to adjust your Virtual Memory settings, specifically the size and location of your paging file. Although your machine will continue to run fine no matter what your settings are, better performance can be achieved in just a few steps. Here are some quick rules to follow:

❋ Your paging file should be stored on its own drive, if possible

❋ If a separate drive for the paging file is not available, store the paging file on the data drive, not the boot drive

❋ Set the minimum and maximum page file sizes to the same value

❋ Make the page file 1.5 to 2 times the value of your RAM

To change your page file settings, do the following:

1. Open the Control Panel.
2. Double-click on the System icon.
3. Click the Advanced tab in the System Properties dialog box.
4. Click the Settings button in the Performance section.
5. Click the Advanced tab in the Performance Options dialog box.
6. Click the Change button in the Virtual Memory section.
7. In the Virtual Memory dialog box (see Figure 1.7), do the following:

    ❋ Select the drive where you want the paging file to be stored.

    ❋ Select the Custom Size option.

    ❋ Set the minimum and maximum size values.

8. Click the Set button.
9. Click OK.

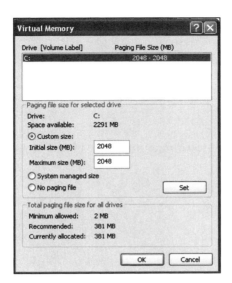

Figure 1.7
The Virtual Memory dialog box.

Using .ini Variables to Customize the Track View

If you find the order of the Track view controls don't meet your needs, you can change their order using a variable in the cakewalk.ini file. The following two tips cover ways to change the Track view.

Changing the Order of Track Pane Controls

When you are trying to squeeze as many tracks in the Track view as possible, you might want to move the controls around. The order of the controls in the Track pane is determined by a set of .ini file variables that can be changed using Notepad or any text editor. Use this procedure to do so:

1. Using Windows Explorer, navigate to the directory where you installed SONAR 5.
2. Locate the cakewalk.ini variable and open it in Notepad or whatever text editor you prefer.
3. Add the following lines to the file if you want to change the order of the audio track controls:

```
[Audio Widgets]
W0=Volume
W1=Pan
W2=Trim
```

```
W3=Input
W4=Output
W5=FX
W6=Aux
W7=Phase
W8=Interleave
```

4. **And these lines if you want to change the order of MIDI track controls:**

```
[MIDI Widgets]
W0=Volume
W1=Pan
W2=Trim
W3=Input
W4=Output
W5=Channel
W6=Bank
W7=Patch
W8=Key
W9=Time
W10=FX
W11=Chorus
W12=Reverb
```

5. **Reorder the controls to suit your needs; for example:**

```
[Audio Widgets]
W0=Volume
W1=Pan
W2=FX
W3=Output
W4=Input
W5=Trim
W6=Aux
W7=Phase
W8=Interleave
```

6. **If you are having any problems, check for typos.**

Force Controls to Remain in the Track Header

If you are always looking for more room in the Track view, you can force track controls to remain in track headers even when they are not minimized. By default, the track headers do not display any controls when you are zoomed out enough to show any in the body of the Track pane (see Figure 1.8).

Figure 1.8

Track header before editing the .ini file.

1. Using Windows Explorer, navigate to the directory where you installed SONAR 5.
2. Locate the cakewalk.ini variable and open it in Notepad or whatever text editor you prefer.
3. Add the following lines to the file (see Figure 1.9):

   [WinCake]

   TVWidgetsStickInHeader=1

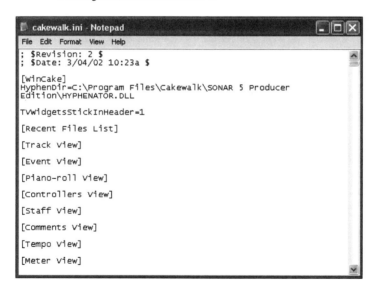

Figure 1.9

The line TVWidgetsStick InHeader line in the Cakewalk.ini file.

The result looks like Figure 1.10.

Figure 1.10

Track header after editing the .ini file.

Creating a Quiet Computer Environment

Recording audio requires quiet, but computers can be very noisy pieces of equipment. You can either shield your microphones from the computer by placing them in separate rooms like in a traditional studio, or even a bedroom with a closet, or you can quiet your PC. The following list shows the noise sources of computers and discusses what you can do to reduce or eliminate the problem:

❊ Case fans—There might be one or several of these. These can be replaced with fans that are larger but spin at a slower rate.

❊ Heat sink fan—The fan that draws the heat away from your CPU heat sink and fan is critical. It can be replaced with a quieter fan.

❊ Hard drives—Unfortunately, the very thing that makes a hard drive faster (RPM) also makes it louder. There are models that are quieter than others; silentpcreview.com is a great resource for which models are quietest.

❊ Hard drive coolers—hard drive coolers can help reduce noise. They are particularly effective when using a RAID setup. A proper system cooling and ventilation via appropriate intake and exhaust fans allow components to run cooler, which is typically quieter. Many high-end DAWs use the Nexus Drive-A-Way (http://www.nexustek.nl/ driveaway.htm).

Creating a Foolproof Backup System

Losing data is unacceptable and if it happens once, that is once too often. You need to create a backup strategy so that none of your recording, sequencing, mixing, or mastering efforts are wasted due to a faulty hard drive. How often you back up is up to you, but after every session is not extreme, especially if you have put in a long session.

Back up to a USB, FireWire, removable hard drive, DVD drive, or CD drive after every session. If this seems like too much work, save each project you have worked on to your boot drive as a Cakewalk bundle file (extension .cwb), assuming you have two drives. This guards against complete hard drive failure, at the very least. Once a week, copy all projects to your preferred backup medium: DVD-R/RW, CD-R, external hard drive, or even tape. The method you use is less important than actually doing it and doing it regularly.

At the end of every milestone—a CD, movie score, jingle, and so on—make two DVD-R or CD-R backups of all the work and store one in a safe place in your own home or studio. Store the second copy in a place other than where your studio is. If your studio is in your home, send your backups to a family member or friend you can trust who is aware of their importance. This safeguard protects you from a fire or other disaster in your studio and provides another level of safety.

Having a bunch of discs around is not enough. Make sure you write down what is on each disc and why it is important.

To make the transfer of your audio projects easier, make sure you are using per-project Audio in SONAR. With every project in its own self-contained directory, backing up your data is as easy as dragging and dropping.

Cakewalk files authored long before SONAR replaced Pro Audio can still be opened in SONAR 5. So, it is safe, for the time being at least, to save your data as project files and wave files. For the long haul, however, it is best to save your files, at least the ones you can't live without, in more than one format. One other option is to save your projects as OMF files. Another is to save each of the tracks in your project as a broadcast wave file. Broadcast wave files are the same as wave files, but they have the added bonus of knowing their start time, so in a worst-case scenario, you can rebuild your entire project by importing each track one at a time without having to line everything up again.

To keep everything in one place, you might want to freeze all your virtual instruments and MIDI tracks.

Don't forget, during the process of backing up all your data, to back up your instrument definitions, video, and anything else you can think of. You'll sleep better at night if you do.

Besides your audio data and SONAR projects, you may also want to back up your system files. A good way to do that is to use Norton Ghost which allows you to take a snapshot of your system and stores it as a disk image.

Synchronizing Multiple Digital Connections

If you've ever had your various digital connections lose synch with each other, you know how frustrating it can be. Use a reliable timing master, either standalone, or one of your audio interfaces, and have the rest of your system slave to it.

1. Pick a timing master (different quality clocks will produce more or less jitter, which can affect high-end frequencies and stereo imaging). Experiment to find the best clock source in your system.

2. Attach cables (optical cables must never be bent at an angle).

3. Most hardware can obtain clock from S/PDIF optical—you can also use a Wordclock device separately. You can improve the sound of slaved devices even if no digital connections are present if one of your devices has an inferior clock.

4. Set your audio interface's clock to external—also used for using multiple soundcards locked together.

5. Make sure SONAR is set to the sample rate of the hardware (most often 44.1 or 48).

Customizing Your SONAR Toolbars

If toolbars are taking up too much room at the top of SONAR, you can hide the ones you don't use by choosing Views > Toolbars from the SONAR menu and unchecking the toolbars you don't want to see (see Figure 1.11). For example, if you are not using looping, markers, or editing MIDI, hiding the Looping, Markers, and Inline Piano Roll toolbars makes a lot of sense. To see how few you need, try starting with only the Transport toolbar and adding others as you need them. You might be surprised how few you actually use on a regular basis, and how much room you can save by hiding those you don't need.

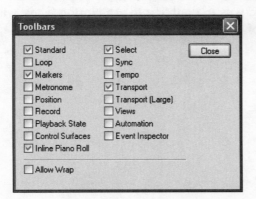

Figure 1.11

The Toolbars dialog box.

You can move toolbars by clicking and dragging them to a new location. Toolbars can be floated or moved to the sides or bottom of SONAR, as shown in Figure 1.12.

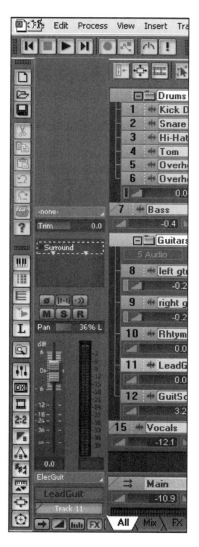

Figure 1.12

Toolbars on the top and left.

Using Your Old Sequencer's Key Bindings

One of the most difficult aspects of using a new application is the new keyboard shortcuts you have to learn. But now, you can import your favorite key bindings from Pro Tools, Cubase, Digital Performer, Nuendo, Vegas, Logic, and Samplitude using the Key Bindings dialog box. To do so:

1. Choose Options > Key Bindings from the SONAR menu.

2. In the Key Bindings dialog box, click the Import button (see Figure 1.13).

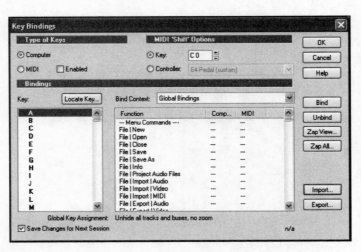

Figure 1.13
Key Bindings dialog box.

3. In the Import Key Bindings dialog box, select a .kbn file (see Figure 1.14) and click Open.

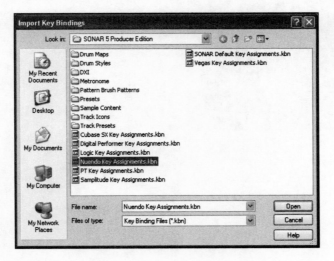

Figure 1.14
Import Key Bindings dialog box.

Creating Custom Track Icons

Sometimes the content of a track isn't readily apparent based on the track's name. You can make it a little easier to identify the exact track you want by using track icons. There are many preset icons that come with SONAR, but you can make your own, perhaps adding a personal touch to each project. The default track icons are located in a folder where you installed SONAR, called Track Icons.

You must save the files as bitmap files (extension .bmp) to be recognized by SONAR. Ideally, your icons should be 128 by 128 pixels, but SONAR will scale a graphic to size. Right-click the default track icon and choose Load Track Icon from the menu that appears to locate a Track Icon file. Figure 1.15 shows two tracks with track icons.

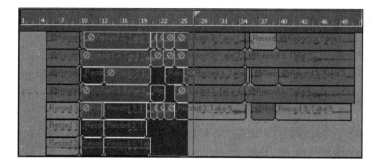

Figure 1.15

Two tracks with track icons.

Instantly Creating Tracks with Pre-Configured Settings

You no longer need to spend your time configuring tracks after you create them. Do it once for each configuration and save it as a preset. You never have to do it again. Track presets can save the following track settings:

* Track name
* Audio or MIDI track
* Input
* Output destination
* Mute, solo, and arm settings
* Bus sends, including volume and pan
* Track parameters
* Track icons
* Effects
* MIDI instrument, including bank and patch

Use this procedure to create a track preset:

1. Configure the track exactly as you want the track preset to be.
2. Choose File > Export > Track Preset from the SONAR menu.
3. In the Save As dialog box, type a name for the preset (be very descriptive, especially if you plan to create a lot of presets), and click OK.

To recall any preset, simply right-click in the Track pane, select Insert > Preset > *preset name* from the menu that appears (see Figure 1.16).

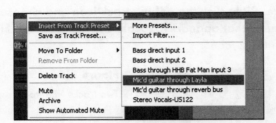

Figure 1.16

Inserting a track preset.

Improving Transport Control Performance

If you find your Transport Controls freeze momentarily on Stop, you can improve the performance by unchecking the Zero All Controllers on Stop option in the Project Options dialog box's MIDI Out tab (see Figure 1.17). This is a built-in sort of MIDI Panic button which is on by default. If you do not do much with MIDI or don't experience stuck notes when you do use MIDI, this option does not need to be checked and your Transport will be more responsive.

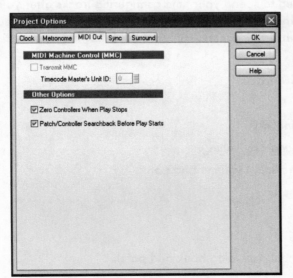

Figure 1.17

The Project Options dialog box's MIDI Out tab.

Adding Applications to the Tools Menu

Some audio editors show up automatically in the Tools menu. Some do not. There is a free utility called Sonar Utils by Bruce Ennis (http://bruce-ennis.com: 8085/download.htm) that allows you to add an application to the SONAR Tools menu. The following steps show you how to use it to add an application to the Tools menu. (In this case, you're adding the free wave editor called Audacity, available from www.sourceforge.net, to the Tools menu.) Make sure you close SONAR before beginning.

1. Download and install Sonar Utils from http://bruce-ennis.com:8085/ download.htm.

2. Click the Tools Menu tab at the bottom of Sonar Utils.

3. Right-click in the big, white field below the text *Tools Menu* (see Figure 1.18).

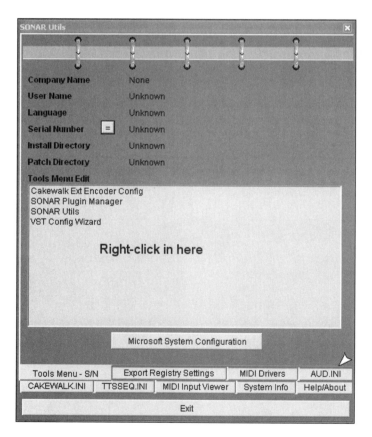

Figure 1.18

Right-click to open the Tools Menu dialog box.

4. In the Tools Menu dialog box, click the button to the right of the Exe Path field.

5. In the File Open dialog box, use the Directory field to navigate to the folder where your editor is located. Select the .exe file in the Name field and click Open (see Figure 1.19).

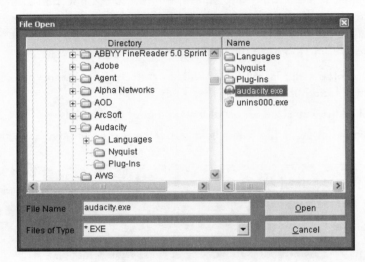

Figure 1.19

The File Open dialog box in Sonar Utils.

6. The File Open dialog box closes and the Tools Menu dialog box is now populated with the editor's data (see Figure 1.20).

7. Choose WaveEditor from the Type drop-down menu.

8. Click Add/Update.

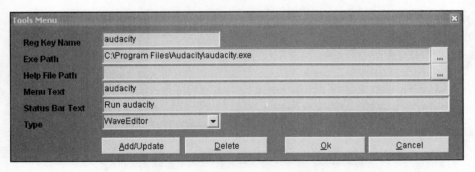

Figure 1.20

The Tools Menu dialog box in Sonar Utils.

Quickly Sorting Tracks by Channel or Output

If your project has a lot of tracks, you might find it hard to immediately find the ones that share the same output, channel, or even track status. You can quickly sort your tracks to group them for quick changes to new busses, MIDI channels, or hardware outputs. To do so:

1. Choose Track > Sort from the SONAR menu (see Figure 1.21).

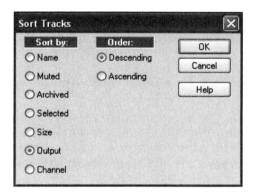

Figure 1.21

Sort Tracks dialog box.

2. In the Sort Tracks dialog box, choose from the following options to sort a track by:

   ❀ Name

   ❀ Muted

   ❀ Archived

   ❀ Selected

   ❀ Size

   ❀ Output

   ❀ Channel

3. Select Ascending or Descending and click OK.

Restoring Corrupted Projects

Failure to open a project is frustrating, but there are a few methods you can use to recover your projects and their data.

Using Safe Mode to Open a Corrupted Project

At some point you may try to open a project you have spent a lot of time editing only to have SONAR crash or issue an error message. Before you panic and blow away any edits made since your last backup, try opening the project in Safe Mode. Safe Mode attempts to open your project in the following state:

❄ Only the Track view opens.

❄ Prompts before attempting to load each individual plug-in, Dxi, or VST instrument.

If you suspect a specific plug-in to be the cause, you can allow all the plug-ins except that one to open. If that doesn't do it, open the file with no plug-ins and use the Save As command to save a copy of your project with a new file name.

Do the following to open a project in Safe Mode:

1. Choose File > Open from the SONAR menu.

2. Navigate to where the project is saved.

3. Click on the file to select it and hold down the Shift key while clicking Open.

4. For each DXi, VST, and plug-in, a File Open – Safe Mode dialog box appears asking if you want to open that instance (see Figure 1.22).

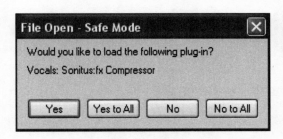

Figure 1.22
File Open—Safe Mode dialog box.

Opening Audio from Corrupted Bundle Files

On some occasions, often due to a drive or media failure, a Bundle file will become so corrupted that SONAR can no longer open it. Whereas a Project file stores the audio separately so that it is still accessible, Bundle (*.CWB) files are monolithic and hence everything is contained in the single file. However, you can often still salvage these projects by using the following steps.

1. Rename the CWB file to a WAV file. If you cannot see file extensions in Windows, open a folder and go to Tools > Folder Options > View. Uncheck Hide Extensions for Known File Types (see Figure 1.23).

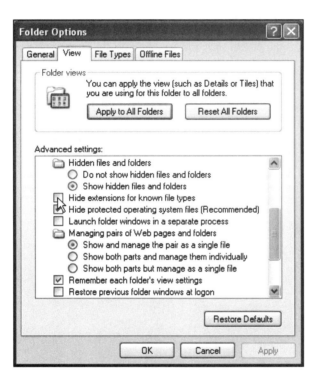

Figure 1.23

The Folder Options dialog box.

2. Load the project into a wave editor or back into SONAR itself. All of the header data will be ignored, and instead SONAR will just look at the contained audio data. All of the tracks in the project will be loaded as a single track, joined end to end.

Fixing a Corrupted Wave File Using a File Editor

After transferring a project or running disk utilities, you might find you cannot open certain audio tracks in a project. You might find that a file exported from another program does not import properly or vice versa, and the exported file from SONAR causes issues. The issue is typically with the file header, not the way the wave is stored. One quick way to fix a corrupted wave file or to resolve file incompatibilities is to use the program called StripWav (http://www.lightlink.com/tjweber/StripWav/StripWav.html).

This application also allows you to remove ACID or groove-clip information that might be causing problems with playback.

2 } Recording

This chapter covers some recording techniques that improve workflow, allowing you to work faster and more efficiently when laying down audio tracks or MIDI data.

One-Hand Step Recording

SONAR 5 has streamlined the step recording process so you can now use one hand to easily make all your step recording commands on your computer keyboard, keeping your other hand free to enter notes on your MIDI controller. The following procedure shows you how to step record with one hand on your computer keyboard and the other hand on your MIDI controller:

1. In a project that has an empty MIDI track, choose Transport > Step Record from the SONAR menu, or press Shift+F4.
2. If necessary, enable Step Recording by clicking the Activate Step Record button at the bottom right of the Step Record dialog box (see Figure 2.1).

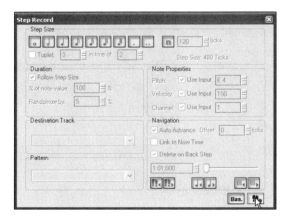

Figure 2.1

The Activate Step Record button in the Step Record dialog box.

3. In the Step Record dialog box (see Figure 2.2), select the track you want to step record in.

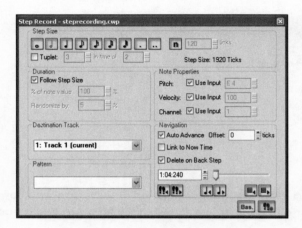

Figure 2.2

Step Record dialog box.

4. Use the Table 2.1 to find the keyboard shortcuts on the Number Pad section of your keyboard for step recording:

Table 2.1 Keyboard Shortcuts for Step Recording

To Do This	Use This Keyboard Shortcut
Set note size to Whole	1 on the Number Pad
Set note size to Half	2 on the Number Pad
Set note size to Quarter	4 on the Number Pad
Set note size to Eighth	8 on the Number Pad
Set note size to 16th	6 on the Number Pad
Set note size to 32nd	3 on the Number Pad
Set note size to 64th	7 on the Number Pad
Make note size selected a dotted note	* on the Number Pad
Add a step size to a previous step	+ on the Number Pad and press the appropriate number for the note size on the Number Pad
Step backwards	0 on the Number Pad
Step forward	Enter on the Number Pad
Move backwards by a measure	Ctrl+0 on the Number Pad
Move forward by a measure	Ctrl+Enter on the Number Pad

5. Enter a note on your MIDI controller.

It won't take long for you to become comfortable with these shortcuts; you'll be step recording quickly.

Step Recording a Groove

Step recording in SONAR using a pattern lets you create a groove without any mistakes faster than you can play it in real-time. For non-piano players looking to create a funky part, this is an ideal solution. A pattern is just a series of numbers and dots, which represent rests. You enter notes one at a time, or in steps, and the rests are skipped giving you a rhythmic pattern. To use pattern step recording:

1. In a project that has an empty MIDI track, choose Transport > Step Record from the SONAR menu.

2. In the Step Record dialog box, select the track you want to step record in (see Figure 2.3).

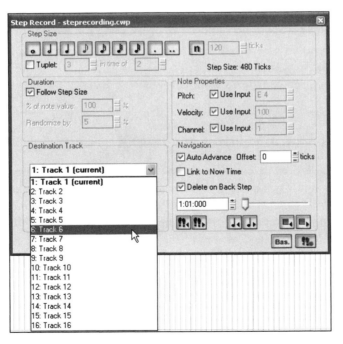

Figure 2.3

Selecting the step record track in the Step Record dialog box.

3. In the Pattern field, enter the groove you want to record. In this example, it is a blues shuffle with the step size set to 8th note triplets (see Figure 2.4).

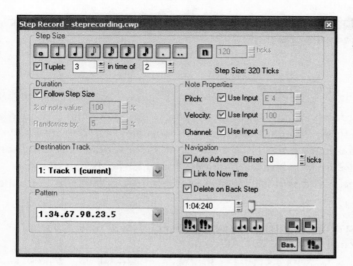

Figure 2.4
A blues shuffle pattern.

4. Use your MIDI controller to enter notes or chords. If you are not using Auto Advance mode, you must manually advance to the next step either in the Step Recording dialog box or by using the keyboard shortcut.

5. Once you've completed the pattern, it returns to the beginning and repeats, so you can record the blues progression faster than you can play it in real-time, and without any timing issues.

Manipulating MIDI Input Using MIDI-OX

MIDI-OX is billed by its creators as the "world's greatest all-purpose MIDI utility," and they'll get no argument from me. The following tips cover just a couple of its many uses. MIDI-OX is a free download for non-commercial use, available from midiox.com. For these tips, you will also need MIDI Yoke, also available as a free download from midiox.com.

Split a MIDI Controller's Input to Multiple Channels

Think of MIDI-OX as a filter that can take any MIDI data and redefine it on its way to and from SONAR. One handy use for a filter like this is to split a MIDI keyboard, or any controller for that matter, into multiple channels so you can record two or more instruments on the same keyboard at the same time. Use the following procedure to record on two channels at the same time using the same MIDI controller:

1. Download and install both MIDI-OX and MIDI Yoke.

2. Open MIDI-OX.

3. Click the Select MIDI Devices to Open button (see Figure 2.5).

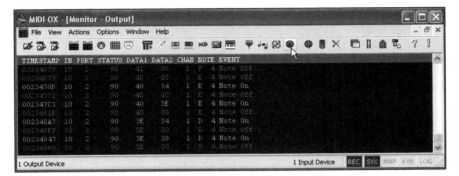

Figure 2.5
The Select MIDI Devices to Open button in MIDI-OX.

The MIDI Devices dialog box appears (see Figure 2.6).

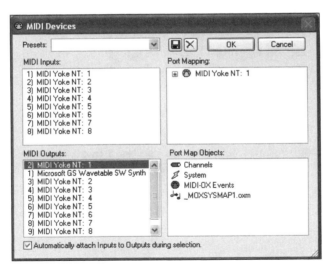

Figure 2.6
MIDI OX's MIDI Devices dialog box.

4. In the MIDI Inputs section, choose your MIDI controller.

5. In the MIDI Outputs section, select a MIDI Yoke driver.

6. Click OK in the MIDI Devices dialog box.

7. Click the MIDI Data Mapping Transforms button (see Figure 2.7) to open the Translation Map dialog box.

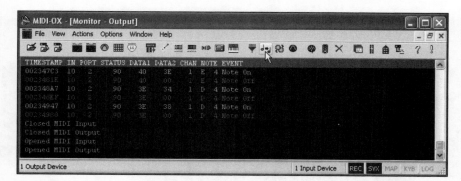

Figure 2.7

The cursor is on the MIDI Data Mapping Transforms button.

8. In the Translation Map dialog box, click the Insert button to open the Define Mapping dialog box (see Figure 2.8).

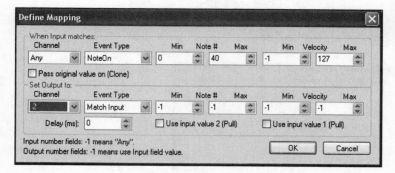

Figure 2.8

The Define Mapping dialog box.

9. Create a range of NoteOn values you want to go to the alternate channel; in this case the lower notes are going to channel 2.

10. Create a range of NoteOff values matching the NoteOn values.

11. Click OK. See Figure 2.9 for how the mapping looks in the Translation Map dialog box.

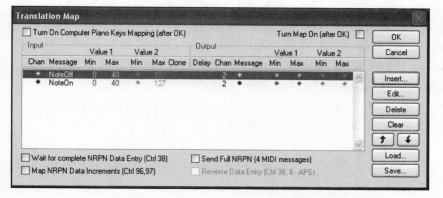

Figure 2.9

The Translation Map dialog box with lower notes sent to channel 2.

12. In SONAR, create two MIDI tracks.

13. Set the input of one of the tracks to the MIDI Yoke driver you set as an output in MIDI-OX on channel 1.

14. Set the input of the other track to the same driver, but on channel 2.

15. Arm both tracks and record, playing the full range of the MIDI controller.

Use Your Computer Keyboard to Play Difficult Chords

MIDI-OX has a feature that lets you play notes, and even chords, using your computer keyboard. By pressing a single key you can play a major, minor, seventh, or even augmented chord. Here's how:

1. Open SONAR and MIDI-OX.

2. Set a MIDI Yoke driver as an output and assign that driver as an input in a track in SONAR.

3. In MIDI-OX, click the Play Notes from the Computer Keyboard button (see Figure 2.10).

Figure 2.10
The Play Notes from the Computer Keyboard button in MIDI-OX.

4. Press the Caps Lock key on your computer's keyboard.

5. Press a key assigned to a root note in Table 2.2 to play a major chord.

Table 2.2 Computer Keys and the Notes They Play

Note	Key
Middle C (MIDI note 60)	Q
C#/Db	S
D	W
D#/Eb	D
E	E
F	R
F#/Gb	G
G	T

(continues)

Table 2.2 Computer Keys and the Notes They Play *(continued)*

Note	Key
G#/Ab	H
A	Y
A#/Bb	J
B	U
C (MIDI note 72)	I

6. If necessary, change the octave range of notes using F2 through F9.
7. Press a key in the Number Pad section of your keyboard to change the type of chord you are playing. See Table 2.3 for the Number Pad keys to play for the various chord types. See Figure 2.11 for an example of MIDI-OX playing a series of major chords.

Table 2.3 Number Pad Keys and the Chords They Specify

Number Pad Key	Type of Chord
Numpad 0	Major
Numpad 1	Inversion
Numpad 2	Second Inversion
Numpad 3	Minor
Numpad 4	Minor Sixth
Numpad 5	Minor Seventh
Numpad 6	Sixth
Numpad 7	Seventh
Numpad 8	Note doubled one octave higher
Numpad 9	Ninth
Numpad /	Diminished
Numpad *	Augmented
Numpad .	Clear

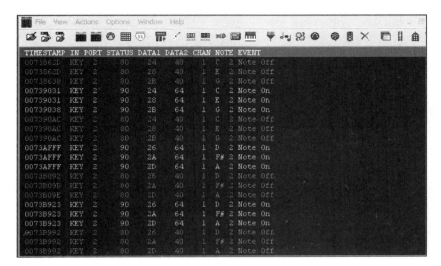

Figure 2.11
MIDI-OX sending major
chord triads.

Creating Multiple Headphone Mixes

One of the first hurdles you will encounter when recording a band is trying to satisfy the desire for individual headphone mixes for each musician. The vocalist wants more vocals. The guitarist wants more guitar. SONAR's bussing flexibility makes it possible to satisfy everyone. The next two tips cover several ways you can create multiple headphone mixes.

A Mix for Each Band Member Using Busses

Busses give you complete control over your mixes and determine what each band member hears while recording. This can be an incredible help when recording multiple players simultaneously. A vocalist might, for example, need to hear a lot of guitar or piano and his or her own vocals, but just enough drums to keep time. For the drummer, the situation might be reversed. If you take a little time to set up multiple mixes using busses, things can go much smoother during the session. Use the following procedure to create multiple headphone mixes using busses:

1. Create a bus for each band member. You are ultimately limited by the number of output pairs you have on your sound card, so if you have fewer stereo pairs than band members, you might need to have several members share a mix. For instance, if you can't give a separate headphone mix to both the bass player and drummer, they might have to share a mix.

2. Label each bus clearly and descriptively, such as "vocal headphone mix" or "Mix for Chuck." See Figure 2.12 for how this might look.

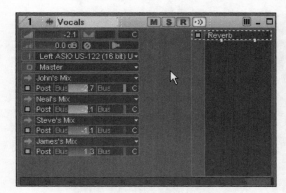

Figure 2.12

A track with four bus sends: one for each headphone mix.

3. Set the outputs for each bus to a different stereo pair (1/2, 3/4, and so on) and connect each stereo pair to a headphone amp. You can use several single headphone amps, or one multiple.

4. In each track, create sends to each of the new busses.

5. Adjust the bus sends in each track to the tastes of each band member.

A Mix for Each Band Member
Using an External Headphone Mixer

If you do not have enough stereo pairs to create a separate mix for each band member using busses in SONAR, you can use an external headphone mixer to at least have some control over each mix. To create multiple headphone mixes using an external headphone mixer, do the following:

1. Connect your sound card outputs or headphone jack to your external headphone mixer. Important note about headphone jacks on sound cards: some sound cards allow you to hear only the channel 1/2 outputs through the headphone jack. If you are not hearing anything through your headphones, make sure your mix is routed to the channel 1/2 output.

2. Use your headphone mixer to adjust volume settings for each member of the band.

Busses and the Metronome

SONAR's metronome is more flexible than ever. You can now send the metronome to any track or bus in your project. This makes using the metronome easier than ever if you find yourself turning it on and off all the time. The following describes a way to turn on or off your metronome with just one click of your mouse:

1. In your project, create a bus for your metronome. Give it an obvious name like Audio Metronome.
2. Choose Options > Project from the SONAR menu.
3. In the Project Options dialog box, click the Metronome tab.
4. In the Audio Metronome section, set your First Beat and Other Beats sounds and dB levels.
5. Set the Output to your Audio Metronome bus.
6. In the General section, check the Recording and Playback check boxes. Your settings in the Metronome tab of the Project Options dialog box should look something like Figure 2.13.

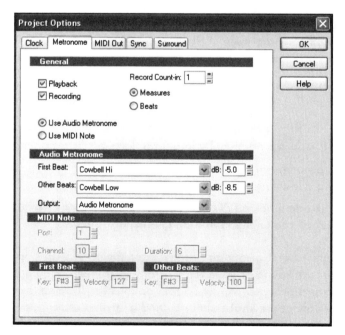

Figure 2.13

The output of the metronome set to the Audio Metronome bus in the Project Options dialog box.

7. If you want to send the metronome only to certain tracks, create sends in the Audio Metronome bus to just those tracks (see Figure 2.14).

Figure 2.14

Sending the audio metronome bus to individual bus mixes.

8. Click the Mute button in the Audio Metronome bus to turn off the metronome.

Overdriving Preamps as an Effect

The emergence of consumer-priced analog preamps in recent years gives anyone the opportunity to add tube warmth to their signal before it is converted to digital audio. The unique sound a piece of tube gear adds to a vocal part can be subtle and distinctive. However, there is no reason it has to be subtle. You can get some unusual special effects by cranking up the gain in your preamp. The following are things you can try to get unusual sounds from a preamp:

❋ Turn down your output volume to avoid damage to your speakers (and ears).

❋ Crank the input gain until you get the level of distortion you want.

❋ Crank the output gain until you get the level of distortion you want.

❋ If your preamp has a compression section, use that to squash the sound by using a low threshold and a sharp knee.

❋ If your preamp has an EQ section, adjust the settings while talking into the microphone until you find an interesting sound.

Most preamps have several gain stages, each giving you an opportunity to further distort the sound of your voice or any instrument. Preamps with EQ and compression sections give you additional options for shaping the sound. Spend some time tweaking the knobs until you find a special effect that works for you. Adding reverb or delay to the signal chain, or after the fact using a plug-in in SONAR, can add a sense of space to the effect.

Creating Perfect Space Impulses

SONAR 5's new Perfect Space plug-in is a great sounding reverb. Perfect Space is a convolution reverb that uses samples. These samples are the responses to an impulse. The impulse response can be from any sound created using a live space or any gear. A sound passes through space, like a hand clap in a room, and generates a response from the walls. The sample of this sound, minus the original sound of the hand clap, defines how the room affects the sound.

There is no need to settle for the impulses included with Perfect Space. You can record your own. Perfect Space uses the sound of an affected signal to process other signals in real-time. The next two tips cover how you can create your own custom impulses.

Using Your External Gear

The beauty of Perfect Space Convolution Reverb is that there is no limit to the number of its possible applications. Any piece of external gear that adds a desired sonic color to your signal is a good candidate for Perfect Space, so it does not have to be a reverb unit, or even an effects processor. It can be a microphone pre-amp or anything that imparts a particular "sound" that you add to an audio signal, like the warmth of a tube unit.

To create a custom impulse from a piece of external gear, use the following procedure:

1. Find a wave file that has a prominent transient, like drum hit or something similar.
2. In SONAR, select a track and choose File > Import > Audio to add the wave file to the track.
3. Set the output port of the track your wave file is on to the one connected to your external gear.
4. Run your external gear's output back into an input.
5. Create a new track and assign its input to the one your external gear is connected to.
6. Arm the new track.
7. Adjust the settings of the external gear as desired.
8. Record the externally processed track.
9. Zoom in on the two tracks.
10. Line them up so that the new track is exactly out of phase with the original (see Figure 2.15). See the tip "Moving Clips in Time to Fix Phase Issues" in Chapter 3 for information on doing this.

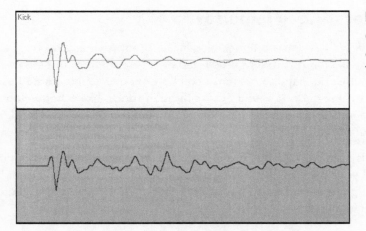

Figure 2.15

Original and processes clips lined up in the Track view.

11. Invert the phase of the new track by clicking the Invert Phase button (see Figure 2.16).

Figure 2.16

The Invert Phase button activated.

12. Listen to the two clips. If you hear any of the original hit, adjust the location of the new track until you do not.

13. Mix the clips down to one clip.

14. Export the clip to a wave file, giving it a descriptive name.

You can now use the clip in Perfect Space as an impulse.

Using a Live Space

Ever wish you could bottle the sound of your living room or bathroom and use it for your drum kit? Now you can. Perfect Space lets you take any space and apply its properties to your music. This is also a very useful tool if you want to re-record a part of a song that was recorded in a room that is now unavailable. To create a Perfect Space impulse from a live room, use the following procedure:

1. In the space you want to model, set up two microphones, one at the "sweet spot" you think sounds the best and the other right next to the source you are going to record. Ideally, these two microphones are not very close to each other.

2. Create two tracks in SONAR and arm both.

3. Route a microphone to each track.

4. Record a sine wave sweep—if you have access to a sine wave generator and very accurate speakers—or a short, loud sound like a hand clap, drum hit, or balloon popping, onto both tracks.

5. In SONAR, line up the two tracks so they are out of phase, or line them exactly and click the Phase button to invert the phase of one of the tracks (see Figure 2.17). The microphone farther from the source will need to be moved back in time by roughly a millisecond per foot farther from the source than the first microphone.

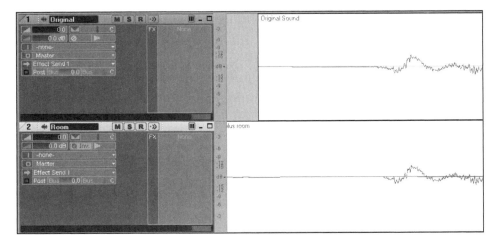

Figure 2.17
Tracks lined up with the second track inverted.

6. Listen to the two clips. If you hear any of the original hit, adjust the location of the new track until you do not.

7. Mix the two clips down to one.

8. Export the mixdown clip to a file, giving it a descriptive name.

The impulse you created is now ready to be used in Perfect Space.

Adjusting Sample Frequency in
Confidence Recording for Better Performance

If you are taxing your computer while recording, and don't want to turn off confidence recording, you can decrease the frequency of samples taken by SONAR to use less CPU. You do so using an .ini variable, like this:

1. Exit SONAR if it is running.

2. Navigate to where you installed SONAR 5.

3. In the SONAR 5 folder, open the cakewalk.ini file using Notepad or any text editor.

4. Add the following line to the section [WINCAKE]:

   `WavePreviewSampleFrequency=5`

   See Figure 2.18.

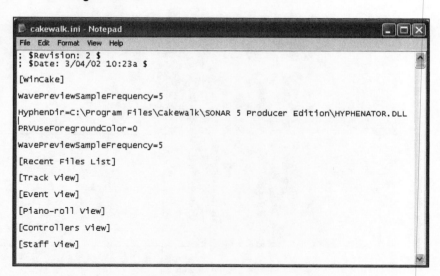

Figure 2.18

The WavePreviewSampleFrequency line added to the Cakewalk.ini file.

5. Save cakewalk.ini.

The acceptable values are between 1 and 10. The larger the number, the fewer samples are taken and the better the performance is.

Improving Meter Performance

The accuracy of meters in SONAR is controlled by a variable in the aud.ini file. Increasing the accuracy of meters increases the demands on your CPU. In the interest of optimum performance without excessive burden on your computer, you can adjust this setting a little at a time until you are satisfied with the result.

The meters in SONAR show the level in a given track or bus at a point in time. You can edit the variable `MeterFrameSizeMS` in the aud.ini file to change how often SONAR reports the level for a track. The default value is 40 milliseconds. Cakewalk recommends a setting of between 10 and 200 milliseconds, although there is no enforced range. To edit this variable, do the following:

1. Navigate to the directory where you installed SONAR.
2. Using Notepad or any text editor, open the file aud.ini.
3. Locate the following line in the `[Wave]` section of aud.ini:

   `MeterFrameSizeMS=40`

   See Figure 2.19.

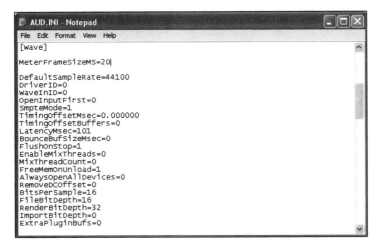

Figure 2.19

The `MeterFrameSizeMS` line edited in the Aud.ini file.

4. Change the value from 40 to anything between 10 and 200. A lower value improves meter performance. A higher value reduces the amount of CPU required for meters.
5. Save aud.ini.

Non-Destructive Recording with External Effects as Inserts

With SONAR's many built-in effects, it might seem odd to talk about using external effects when recording. But there are some distinct advantages of doing so:

* External effects do not use any CPU and therefore allow you to use an effect when you otherwise might not have the power.

* Preference: you may actually prefer your outboard gear for monitoring.

* Real knobs and controls allow you to make adjustments without using a mouse.

Of course, you can run your signal path right through an effect and save the processed signal to your hard drive, but if you want the feel of the effect without having to commit to it, you can use SONAR's flexible bussing to hear the processed signal while recording it clean. To do so:

1. Connect your source to a sound card input. This might be a vocal through a preamp, and then into a sound card.

2. Connect your effect's input to one of your sound card's outputs.

3. Connect your effect's output to one of your sound card's inputs.

4. Create a track to record the source, arm it, and assign the output to None.

5. Create a bus and assign its output to the output your effect is connected to.

6. Create a send in the track you have armed, and send it to the bus you created.

7. Adjust your outboard effect's settings.

8. Record the track.

9. The track is recorded without the effect.

Recording Tracks Remotely Using MIDI Foot Control

If you have a MIDI foot controller, you can use it as a remote control for recording. Using Cakewalk's Generic Control Surface, you can set a sustain message, for example, to begin recording. Here is how you can set up a MIDI controller to record remotely:

1. Connect your MIDI foot controller, through a keyboard, if necessary, to your MIDI input on your sound card or via USB.

2. In SONAR, choose Options > Control Surfaces.

3. In the Control Surfaces dialog box, click the New Control Surface button (see Figure 2.20).

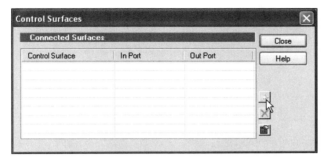

Figure 2.20

The New Control Surface button.

4. In the Control Surface Settings dialog box, select Cakewalk Generic Surface, as in Figure 2.21.

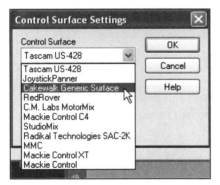

Figure 2.21

Control Surface Settings dialog box.

5. Click OK in the Control Surface Settings dialog box and close the Control Surfaces dialog box.

6. Choose Tools > Generic Control Surface. The Cakewalk Generic Surface dialog box appears. This is where you assign your MIDI input data to commands in SONAR.

7. Choose a command by selecting one of the radio buttons at the bottom of the dialog box.

8. Press a control on your MIDI foot controller (sustain, for example) and press the Learn button in the Cakewalk Generic Surface dialog box.

9. The controller is now mapped to execute that command (see Figure 2.22).

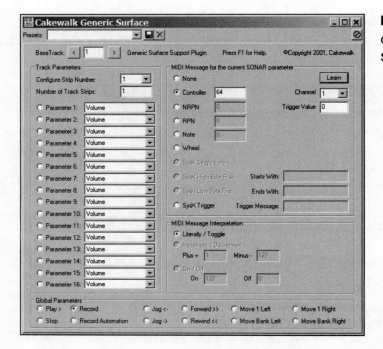

Figure 2.22

Cakewalk Generic Surface dialog box.

10. Repeat for as many commands as you want or have controllers for.

You can now use your foot controller to execute commands away from the computer. This is perfect for recording remotely.

Recording Using Your Computer Keyboard as a Remote Control

Picture yourself in a studio with a soundproof control room, behind a 48 channel mixer that costs more than an average home. You're the producer, instructing your engineer to turn this knob or adjust that fader as the band plays in the studio. If you are like most of us, that isn't reality, but it doesn't mean you can't do the same things all by yourself. SONAR's flexible and powerful key bindings allow you to use your keyboard as a remote control when recording. Learning just a few keyboard shortcuts is all you need to convert your closet or living room into a studio while your computer hums away, loudly, in the room next door. The following is a rough procedure for using your computer keyboard to remotely control recording using SONAR:

1. Add a keyboard cord extension with enough length to move your keyboard to the new location or use a wireless keyboard with enough range.

2. Before moving to the recording location, do the following:

   ❋ If necessary, set up loop recording.

   ❋ Assign any keybindings you want to use.

   ❋ Set up the metronome the way you want it.

3. Move to your remote recording location.
4. Press R to begin recording.
5. Press the spacebar to stop recording.
6. Press W to rewind and start over.

There are many other keybindings and keyboard shortcuts you can use. You can also use a second monitor with a monitor extension cable for a more permanent solution.

Importing Audio from Stand-Alone Recording Devices

If you have been recording at home for more than a few years, chances are you have used more than just a Digital Audio Workstation (DAW) with SONAR. ADATs and hard disk recorders of various types have been around for years. If you have audio on ADAT tape or have saved to a stand-alone hard disk recorder, you can record that into SONAR, and in most cases not lose any quality. The following tips show you how to import your old projects from ADAT and hard disk recorders into SONAR.

Importing ADAT Audio

ADAT machines were the standard for small studios and serious home recordists for a number of years, and just about everyone who laid down tracks during their heyday have ADAT tapes collecting dust on their shelves. If you have ever considered recording those tapes into SONAR, there is no need to wait. It is easy to do. If you don't own an ADAT machine and can't borrow one from a friend, you can find one on eBay at a good price. Check your local music stores to see if they would be willing to rent you one by the day.

ADAT lightpipe is a digital connection designed for use with ADAT machines. Many mid-level sound cards have a lightpipe connection. Lightpipe allows you to record eight channels simultaneously from your ADAT to SONAR.

To record an ADAT using lightpipe:

1. Using an optical cable, connect your ADAT machine to your sound card.

2. Open your sound card's console and show the digital inputs. You might see lightpipe connections listed as ADAT Optical, as in Figure 2.23.

Figure 2.23
ADAT Optical inputs in a sound card console.

3. Make sure all ADAT/lightpipe inputs are unmuted.

4. In SONAR, choose Options > Audio and click the Advanced tab (see Figure 2.24).

5. In the Advanced tab of the Audio Options dialog, select a synchronization option, either Trigger and Freewheel or Full Chase Lock. Note that Full Chase Lock is the more CPU intensive of the two options. Consult your ADAT's manual for the best option.

6. Set the sound card's sample rate to match the ADAT tape's, probably 48kHz.

7. In SONAR, open a new project and set the sample rate to match your ADAT tape's.

8. Create as many tracks as necessary, and set all the inputs to the corresponding digital inputs.

9. Press Record in SONAR.

10. Press Play on the ADAT deck.

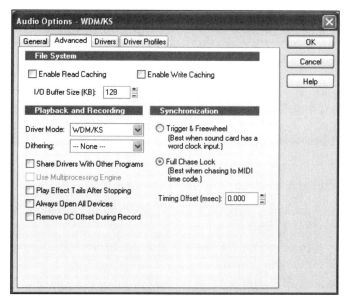

Figure 2.24

The Advanced tab of the Audio Options dialog box.

If your sound card does not have an ADAT optical input, you can record from your ADAT into your sound card's analog inputs. Using this method you will degrade the quality of the audio to some degree. You can limit it by using quality cables connecting the ADAT and sound card.

To record ADAT into analog inputs:

1. If necessary, use RCA to phone adaptors to connect the ADAT deck to your sound card's inputs. Any Radio Shack or electronics store will have the adaptors you need. If you do not have enough inputs to connect all the tracks at once, simply repeat the procedure as many times as necessary.

2. Set the sound card's sample rate to match the ADAT tape's, probably 48kHz.

3. In SONAR, open a new project and set the sample rate to match your ADAT tape's.

4. Create as many tracks as necessary, and set all the inputs to the corresponding analog inputs.

5. Press Record in SONAR.

6. Press Play on the ADAT deck.

If you do not have enough inputs to connect all the tracks at once, simply repeat the procedure as many times as necessary.

Importing Hard Disk Recorder Audio

After the ADAT came the hard disk recorder. The concept is the same as the ADAT, but there is more functionality. Newer models even include CD-RW or DVD-R drives. If you can save your project in a format that SONAR recognizes or track by track, you can use these included drives to import the digital data into SONAR. If not, you have to record it either as a stereo mixdown or track by track using a digital output, usually coaxial or optical. If analog outputs are available, use them only if there are no digital options compatible with your sound card.

To record digital audio from your hard disk recorder:

1. Connect your hard disk recorder to your sound card via a coaxial or optical digital cable.
2. Open your sound card's console and show the digital inputs. Select the digital input type you are using.
3. Make sure all the digital inputs you are using are unmuted.
4. Set the sound card's sample rate to match the hard disk recorder's.
5. In SONAR, choose Options > Audio and click the Advanced tab.
6. In the Advanced tab of the Audio Options dialog, select a synchronization option, either Trigger and Freewheel or Full Chase Lock. Note that Full Chase Lock is the more CPU intensive of the two options. Consult your hard disk recorder's manual for the best option.
7. In SONAR, open a new project and set the sample rate to match the sample rate of your hard disk recorder's project.
8. Create as many tracks as necessary, and set all the inputs to the corresponding digital inputs.
9. If necessary, route all your tracks to the digital outputs. Consult your hard-disk recorder's documentation if you are unsure how.
10. Press record in SONAR.
11. Play back your hard disk recorder's project.

Putting Together a Compact Live Setup

Recording a live show or playing your virtual instruments live are good reasons to take your laptop out into the world, but finding and affording a laptop for recording or powering your software synths is a challenge. The problem is that laptops are made for portability first, performance second. Here are the problems you will encounter when shopping for a laptop DAW:

❄ Slower CPUs—Laptops are always a step behind desktops in CPU performance.

❄ Slower hard drives—Laptops often come with 4200 RPM hard drives.

❄ One, small hard drive—Laptops with two hard drives are rare and the one you get won't be nearly as large as an average desktop drive.

❄ Fewer USB and FireWire ports—Some laptops might not even have both, and the best you can reasonably hope for is two of each.

❄ Fewer audio and MIDI interface options—Most laptops have a single PCMCIA card slot, and some audio hardware companies make PCMCIA interfaces, but you cannot use PCI cards.

❄ Limited number of RAM slots—There are usually just two RAM slots in a laptop.

All of these issues can be solved by taking the time to research your laptop before you buy. Use the following checklist when looking to purchase a laptop:

❄ 7200 RPM hard drive, and two if you are doing multitrack recording.

❄ Get the fastest CPU you can afford. You are already behind on power compared to desktops, so get the fastest chip that fits in your budget.

❄ Get the most RAM you can afford, especially if you plan to use loops or samples. RAM in laptops can be difficult to replace, so you are better off getting enough right up front.

❄ Know your audio and MIDI interface options before you buy your laptop. If you decide to go with a FireWire device after you just bought a laptop that does not have a FireWire port, there isn't all that much you can do.

More and more DAW retailers are adding laptops to their catalog. Buying a laptop DAW that has already been configured saves you a lot of time. These machines also give you features that are hard to find in machines made by the larger laptop manufacturers, like a second hard drive.

If you do choose to go with a laptop from a major manufacturer, look at their gaming machines first. They often have the largest and fastest hard drives the company offers and you know the video card will be powerful enough.

Another option is to think about building a rackmount PC. Rackmounts have many of the benefits of laptops, but can make use of desktop components. You have much more flexibility taking this route. The downside is that a rackmount is bigger and heavier. They also do not run on battery power. If battery power is not necessary and a little extra space and weight are not going to matter, this route is the way to go. A rackmount computer with a rackmount audio and/or MIDI interface will fit nicely in a rack travel case. Racksolutions.com sells a two-space rack drawer with space for a keyboard and LCD monitor.

Here are some tips for getting good results while recording live using SONAR:

❄ Make sure you are not running your computer at its limits, because a drop-out while recording live means you have missed that forever. Overdubs will not sound the same, even if you can get them. Keep your latency reasonable and don't try to record too many tracks at once.

❄ Keep you PC away from obvious dangers like a rowdy crowd and moisture (including beer!), and make sure your cables and power cord aren't likely to be tripped over and pulled out.

❄ Don't try to mic all of the instruments unless you think the sound mix will not be good. A stereo pair, placed strategically, and not too close together, will get you a good sound if the band sounds good.

❄ Turn off Input Monitoring and do not add any effects while recording; doing so only taxes your CPU.

Setting ASIO Driver Latency

ASIO drivers do not follow the latency slider in the Audio Options dialog box. If you want to adjust the latency of your ASIO drivers, use the following procedure:

1. Choose Options > Audio to open the Audio Options dialog box.
2. Click the ASIO Panel button (see Figure 2.25).
3. In the ASIO panel for your sound card (see Figure 2.26), adjust the latency slider to the left to decrease latency.
4. Click OK to close the panel.
5. Click OK to close the Audio Options dialog box.

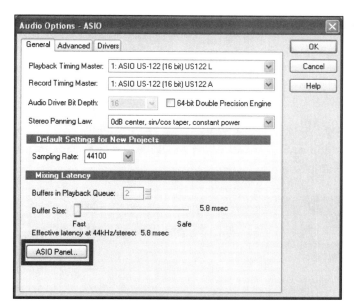

Figure 2.25
The ASIO Panel button in the Audio Options dialog box.

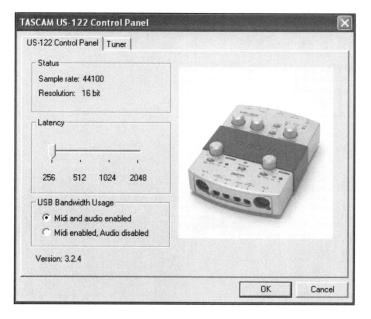

Figure 2.26
The ASIO Panel for the TascamUS-122.

Record MIDI Without Arming a Track

To protect your MIDI data from accidentally being overwritten, SONAR requires you to arm a MIDI track by default. If you want to eliminate the necessity of arming a MIDI track, you can allow MIDI to be recorded without arming a track. To do so:

1. Choose Options > Global from the SONAR menu.
2. Check the option called Allow MIDI Recording without an Armed Track (see Figure 2.27)

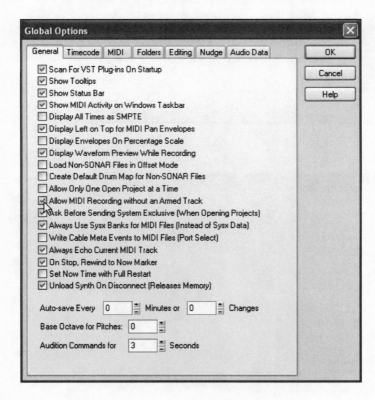

Figure 2.27

The Allow MIDI Recording without an Armed Track option in the Global Options dialog box.

3. Click OK.

Creating Your Own Audio Metronome Sounds

SONAR's audio metronome comes with a range of sounds you can use. But you are not limited to just those sounds. You can create your own. To do so:

1. Locate the wave file you want to use for your metronome sound. Drum or other high-transient sounds stand out best when recording.

2. Save the wave file with a descriptive name, such as Hand Clap.wav or Antique Snare.wav.

3. Copy the file to the Metronome folder in the root directory where you installed SONAR.

4. Open SONAR.

5. Choose Options > Project to open the Project Options dialog box.

6. Click the Metronome tab (see Figure 2.28).

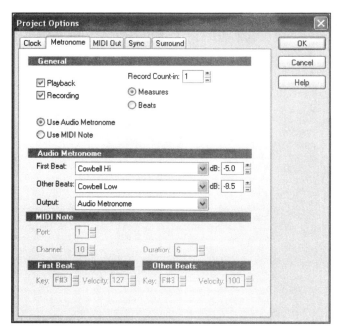

Figure 2.28

The Metronome tab of the Project Options dialog box.

7. Click the Audio Metronome radio button.

8. The new metronome sound is available via the drop-down menus in the Audio Metronome section (see Figure 2.29).

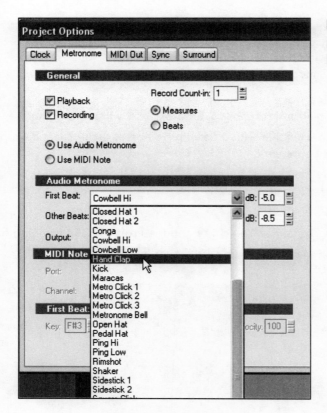

Figure 2.29
New metronome sound in the
First Beat drop-down menu.

3 } Editing Audio

This chapter is all about helping you refine your editing skills. Most SONAR users know the basic audio editing commands and features. In this chapter, you learn the secrets of getting great loops, some tricks for making tracks stand out in a mix, and some tips for editing clips.

Moving Clips in Time to Fix Phase Issues

Having two tracks out of phase with each other creates a diminished signal. In fact, if you clone a track in SONAR, and then click the Invert Phase button on one of them, you hear nothing. This happens because the two waveforms add up to zero, which is silence. Although that is an extreme example, phase problems can cause a lot of frustration while you are mixing.

Phase problems are common when micing drum tracks because of the number of microphones used. The tracks examined here are taken from a snare track and a hi-hat track, where there is a lot of snare bleeding into the hi-hat mic.

1. Stack the two tracks in question next to each other in the Track view (see Figure 3.1).

Figure 3.1
Two clips stacked in Track view.

2. Expand both tracks so together they take up the entire Track view (see Figure 3.2).

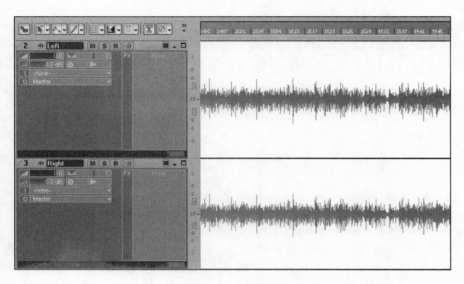

Figure 3.2
Two clips expanded in Track view.

3. Zoom in horizontally until you can see multiple zero-crossings.

4. Compare the two waveforms.

Do they line up? Are they inverted? Something in between?

In the example shown in Figure 3.3, the snare and hi-hat are out of phase with each other.

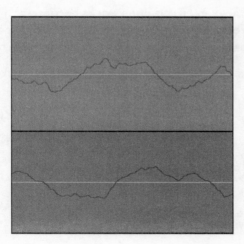

Figure 3.3
Hi-hat and snare tracks out of phase.

There are two excellent ways to fix this issue in SONAR. The Invert Phase button in each track is the easiest solution. Try this first. In the previous example, you invert the phase of the hi-hat track and listen back.

The other solution is to move one of the tracks in time so the two waveforms line up properly. This method gives you greater flexibility and permanently fixes the issue.

Simply drag the bottom clip until it lines up with the top clip, as shown in Figure 3.4.

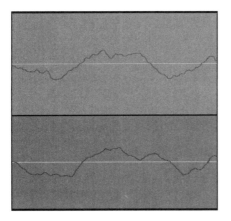

Figure 3.4

Two clips are now in phase with each other.

Eliminating Clicks and Pops when Editing Clips

The best way to prevent clicks and pops when editing clips is to make sure the Snap to Audio Zero Crossings option is checked in the Snap to Grid dialog box or press Shift+N on your computer keyboard to open the Snap to Grid dialog box. This option is on by default. That should fix most problems. However, some edits need a bit of massaging to get rid of an unwanted pop or click.

This procedure works whether you are using track layers or working in multiple tracks.

1. After you have identified an edit that clicks or pops (or makes any kind of undesirable sound), zoom in on the two clips you are trying to edit together.

2. Extend the length of each clip just a bit (the exact amount is a matter of discretion—start with a fraction of a beat, and if at the end of this procedure, there is still an undesirable noise at the transition, go back to this step and adjust the lengths of the overlapping clips). See Figure 3.5.

SONAR 5 Overdrive!

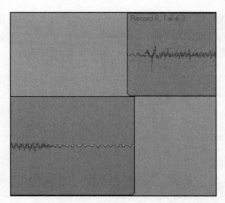

Figure 3.5

Clips with a small overlap.

3. In the Track view, click the down arrow to the right of the Automatic Crossfades button to view the crossfade options (see Figure 3.6).

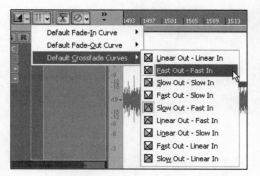

Figure 3.6

The Automatic Crossfades menu.

4. Select a crossfade style. I find that linear-linear works fine, but sometimes you need Fast-Slow for this kind of edit.

5. Click the Automatic Crossfades button to enable it. It appears highlighted when on.

6. Hold the Shift key down (the Shift key preserves the time of the clip, preventing it from moving left or right) while dragging one of the clips on top of the other (see Figure 3.7).

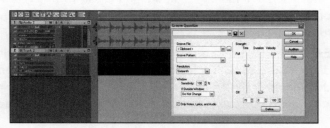

Figure 3.7

Overlapping clips with crossfade.

The two clips now appear with a crossfade. Listen back to hear if the unwanted pop or click is gone.

Customizing the Nudge Command

The Nudge command is a good way to make quick edits on a clip with exact precision. What makes this feature even cooler is its flexibility. You can customize it to meet your needs. Nudge is really three different commands: Nudge 1, Nudge 2, and Nudge 3. Tables 3.1 through 3.3 list some recommended settings for the three nudge features.

Table 3.1 Using the Nudge Command for Remixing

Nudge Command	Type	Value
Nudge 1	Musical Time	Quarter note
Nudge 2	Musical Time	Half note
Nudge 3	Musical Time	Whole note

Remixing is usually centered on beats, most often quarter notes. Being able to jump by quarter, half, and whole note intervals quickly is very handy. If you are working with smaller note divisions, you might want to assign one nudge command to eighth notes instead of whole notes.

Table 3.2 Using the Nudge Command for Video

Nudge Command	Type	Value
Nudge 1	Absolute Time	1 Frame
Nudge 2	Absolute Time	1 Second
Nudge 3	Absolute Time	some number of frames or seconds

When working with video you are often trying to match your audio to a frame or a short section of video. Having one nudge command set to a single frame allows you to move frame by frame. Other nudge settings can be tweaked according to your preferences.

60

SONAR 5 Overdrive!

Table 3.3 Using the Nudge Command for Audio Editing

Nudge Command	Type	Value
Nudge 1	Absolute Time	10 milliseconds
Nudge 2	Absolute Time	20 milliseconds
Nudge 3	Absolute Time	2 or 5 milliseconds

Start with these and see if they work for you. Adjust them to suit your needs. Use the following procedure to customize the three Nudge commands:

1. Choose the Options > Global menu command.
2. Click the Nudge tab (see Figure 3.8).

Figure 3.8

The Nudge tab in the Global Options dialog box.

3. Select Musical Time, Absolute Time, or Follow the Snap Grid for each of the three Nudge commands.

Doubling Tracks for Effect

If you have a thin guitar sound, or a vocal that is not cutting through the mix, a little delay does a lot to thicken a track. Two tracks with less than about 25 to 30 ms of delay between them sound like one thick track to the human ear.

The maximum amount of delay before the tracks separate into two distinct sections varies depending on the source material. Percussion tracks and other high transient sounds tend to allow for only short delay times, whereas sounds that ring out like a strummed guitar or strings tend to allow for longer delay times.

You can use a delay plug-in to fatten a track, but let's make a copy of the track for this example. Using a cloned track, and using Nudge to move the data inside the track, gives you a lot of freedom and is more intuitive than fiddling with knobs to get the same effect. Also, it allows you to add effects to one of the tracks quickly.

1. Right-click on the track you want to fatten.
2. Choose the Clone Track command from the menu that appears.
3. In the Clone Track dialog box (see Figure 3.9), set the Starting Track to the number right below the original.

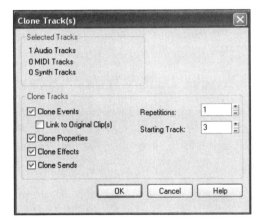

Figure 3.9

The Clone Track(s) dialog box.

4. Make sure the Clone Events option is selected and click OK.
5. Pan the original and the cloned track to opposite sides of the center. If you think you want to put the tracks in different spots in the stereo field, do that now, because tracks separated in the mix tend to need less time separation to achieve the same effect.
6. Set one of the Nudge commands to 5 or 10 ms Absolute Time.
7. Select all the clips in the track and use the Nudge command to move all the clips in the cloned track to the right (later in time) by 10 or 20 ms.

Listen to the song and experiment with different delay times.

Another cool thing you can do with cloned tracks is add an effect, like reverb, to one of the tracks while leaving the other one dry.

Making Precise Clip Splits

Sometimes it is hard to tell exactly where it is best to split a clip, especially at low volume levels where the waveform is hard to see, but you can magnify the waveform of a clip without changing the height of the track using the Audio Scale ruler located between the Track pane and the Clips pane in the Track view. Click and drag on the Audio Scale ruler to zoom in on a waveform, as shown in Figure 3.10.

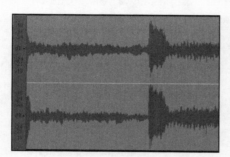

Figure 3.10

Audio Scale ruler is to the right of the Clips pane.

Quickly Comping Vocal Tracks Using Track Layers

Lead vocal tracks rarely come together in one or even several takes. Sometimes you have to piece them together from a bunch of takes. The quickest and easiest way to do that is by using loop recording, keeping all takes in one track with layers showing.

Make sure you feel you've got at least one or two good takes for each major section (verse, chorus, bridge, and so on). After you've recorded your vocals, it is time to select the best parts. You do it by first listening to each take to find the parts you *don't* like. When you find a section, big or small, that isn't up to your standards, simply use the Split tool and cut the clip before and after the undesirable part. After you've done that, you can select the clip and press the Q key to mute it. After you've gone through each take, your track might look something like Figure 3.11.

Figure 3.11

Multi-layered track with some clips muted.

Now that you have deleted the bad stuff, you can compare the good clips to each other to find the best of each. Track layers provide a lot of flexibility when comping a take. New in SONAR 5 is the capability to create new track layers. You can also stack clips in one single layer. You are going to use this new feature to create two new layers, creating two comped tracks. After you've done this, you are going to use the track layer's Mute and Solo buttons to select which layer you hear.

1. Create a new layer by right-clicking between the layer mute and solo buttons and choosing Insert Layer from the menu that appears, as shown in Figure 3.12.

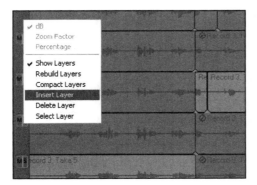

Figure 3.12

Insert Layer command.

2. Hold the Shift and Ctrl keys down while dragging clips to form the first comp layer. The Shift key preserves the start time of the clip, whereas the Ctrl key copies the clip.

3. Repeat the same step for the second comp track. You should have something like Figure 3.13.

4. Now you can listen to each of the comp tracks by clicking the Solo button for that layer. Notice that each of the other track layers is automatically muted when a layer is soloed (see Figure 3.14).

If you want to compare comps that cover more than one layer, simply solo the layers you want to hear.

Another useful tool when comping tracks is the Overlap Cropping tool. If you have clips on bordering layers that overlap, you can use this tool to eliminate the overlap for both clips, as shown in Figures 3.15 and 3.16.

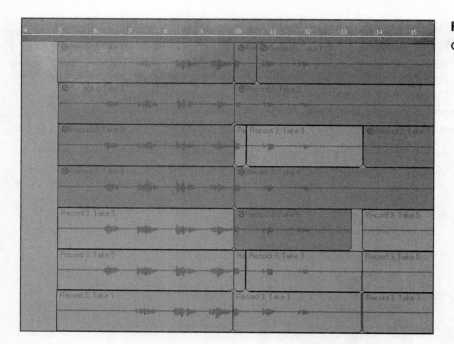

Figure 3.13
Composite tracks.

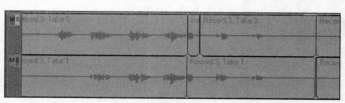

Figure 3.14
Soloed layers.

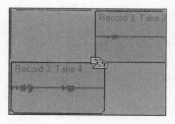

Figure 3.15
Overlap Cropping tool and two uncropped clips.

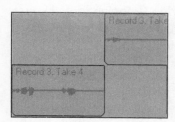

Figure 3.16
Clips cropped.

Eliminating Imperfections Using the Mute Tool

So you nailed a vocal take. You got all the words right, the timing was on, and, best of all, it is a passionate and moving performance. Then you listen back and hear very loud "in" breaths before many of the phrases. You immediately think of how long it'll take to split the clips and mute each offending breath. But the Mute tool gives you a much quicker way to fix this problem.

1. Maximize the track to give yourself enough room to work (see Figure 3.17).

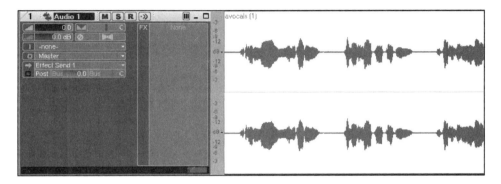

Figure 3.17

A maximized vocal track.

2. Use Horizontal zoom to the point where each phrase appears as a distinct part of the waveform (see Figure 3.18).

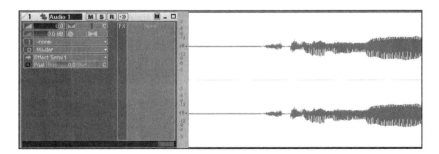

Figure 3.18

A maximized vocal track, zoomed in horizontally.

3. Solo the track.
4. Rewind and begin listening to the track.

5. Press the spacebar to stop when you hear something you want to mute.

6. Click the Mute tool on the Track view toolbar or press the K key to change the cursor to the Mute tool.

7. Drag the Mute tool over the offending section (see Figure 3.19).

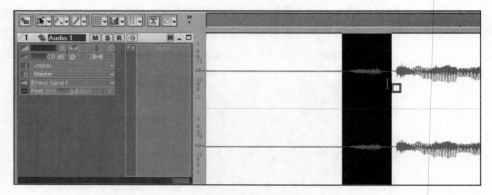

Figure 3.19
Using the Mute tool.

If you mute too much of the clip, just hold the Ctrl key down while using the Mute tool to unmute that section.

Splitting Multiple Clips Simultaneously

A keyboard shortcut that comes in handy when you want to mute an intro or outro is the S key. The Split command works at the Now Time on the current (selected) track. If you select multiple tracks, pressing the S key splits all of the tracks. Figure 3.20 shows two clips split at the same point in time.

For best results, zoom in when moving the Now Time to where you want to split the clips.

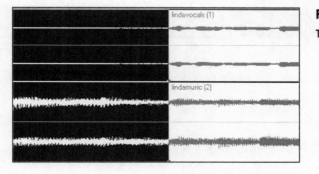

Figure 3.20
Two clips split at the same point.

Creating Great Groove Clips

The capability to create your own Groove clips (Cakewalk's version of ACIDized wave files) gives you a lot of flexibility. That difficult guitar riff only needs to be recorded correctly once and suddenly you have a whole track! On the whole, working with Groove clips is pretty straightforward, but there are a few guidelines you can follow to get the best possible results.

You might not need to make any adjustments to a Groove clip containing drum material, especially if it is a straight beat. However, slowing down a drum loop too much will give you artifacts that sound like echoes. The default settings in the Loop Construction view might work fine on this type of clip. These transient markers mark the points at which the timing of the clip is maintained. To get the most out of percussive loops, make sure the transient sliders are lined up correctly with the clip's transients. Figures 3.21 and 3.22 show you a clip with transient markers properly lined up, and one with misaligned transient markers.

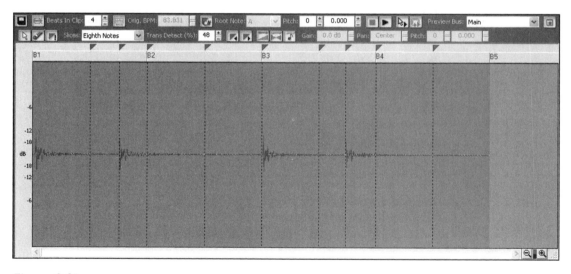

Figure 3.21

Groove clip with transient markers placed properly.

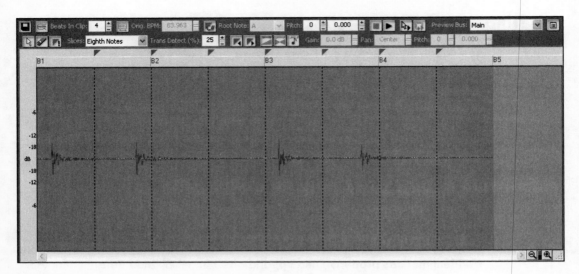

Figure 3.22

Groove clip with transient markers misaligned.

Clips that contain swells and other subtle transient data are much trickier. In some cases, you are limited in the degree of tempo change you can make with these types of clips. For working with clips that have more subtle transients, pay close attention to the tip "Preserving Essential Material."

Preparing Audio for Looping

It might go without saying, but some material lends itself better to looping than others. That's not to say that you can't create a good looped Synth Pad, but it might take some more tweaking and be more sensitive to tempo/key changes than a loop from a drum machine.

Before looping a piece of music, you should check the following:

* Volume—If the recording is quiet, you should increase the gain by using Process > Audio > Normalize or Gain (see Figure 3.23). If this brings up the noise floor too much or the material was heavily compressed, you might try using an Expander plug-in to increase the dynamics.

* Stereo vs. Mono—You can, of course, create loops that are stereo or mono. However, if a loop's left and right channel are radically different, consider bouncing the track down to two separate mono tracks and looping then independently. If there is bleed between the two channels, this could cause phasing issues, so you might have to experiment to see which method works better. You can also sum the loop to a mono loop instead.

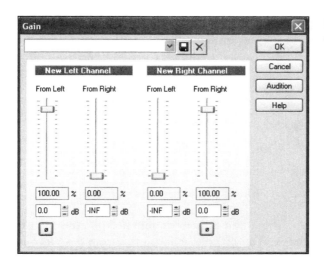

Figure 3.23

The Gain dialog box.

✻ Start Time—It will be easier to check the accuracy of a loop by first trimming any excess space or transients from the beginning. After this is done, you can position the clip so that it starts on the measure. Keep in mind that the first beat of some loops does not happen on the one—if this is the case, be sure to leave the appropriate space in the clip. For an example of this, see Figure 3.24.

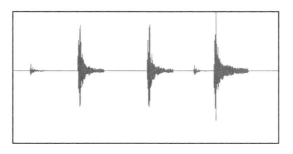

Figure 3.24

A loop with no transient at the first beat.

✻ End Time—Once the clip is lined up to the measure, trim the end to the nearest beat or measure boundary. You can use the Snap settings to help you accomplish this (Shift+N). If the loop doesn't line up exactly, adjust the tempo until the measure boundaries line up with the end point properly.

✻ Sanity Check—At this point, you should be able to select the appropriate number of beats in the time line, set the transport to loop, and hear an accurate representation of what the final loop should sound like. If not, go back to trim or adjust the loop some more.

❋ Apply Trimming/Bounce Clip—If you've only edited out sections of the audio, be sure to use Edit > Apply Trimming. If you've added space to the beginning or end of the clip, you need to use Edit > Bounce to Clip.

❋ Looping—Select the clip and press Ctrl+L to turn it into a Groove clip.

Preserving Essential Material

There are two things that transient markers do:

❋ Preserve the timing at the marker point

❋ Preserve the material on either side of the marker

By default, you should be able to double-click the loop to open the Loop Construction view. You can also choose this from the View menu. SONAR will have selected automatically a set of transients to define how the different *slices* are expanded or compressed when you change the project tempo. It is likely, however, that these slice points are not quite ideal. Figure 3.25 shows a clip with default transient markers in the Loop Construction view.

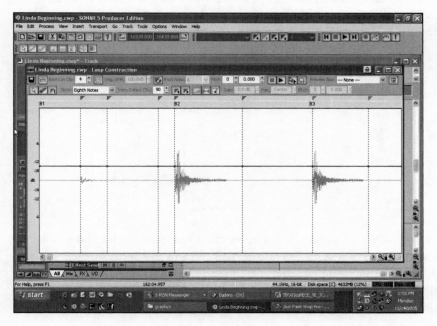

Figure 3.25

A clip with default transient markers in the Loop Construction view.

To begin, reduce the Slices setting to quarter or eighth notes. Then bring the Trans Detect % down to 0%. You will see that your loop is now only broken up into 4 or 8 slices. If you are using a sound like a Synth Pad, you might want to reduce the Slices setting even further. For most drums, arpeggios, or rhythmic loops, this will suffice. Now increase the Transient sensitivity amount and you'll see new slice markers being dropped in. When you see slice markers being added in places where there is no definite drum hit or note, back the amount down a little. The object is to use the bare minimum of slices and to avoid slicing empty space completely. You also should make sure that each hit or note has an associate slice; otherwise, you'll hear flamming or stutters when you start to change the tempo of the project. Finally, manually move, erase, or add slices to accomplish this. The Loop Construction view toolbar provides dedicated tools for this task. Also, double-clicking above the loop will add a new Slice Marker. Slice Markers are red by default; purple if they've been added or edited.

If you want the loop to respond to key information via markers, you need to assign a root to the loop. The root can be any note you choose, but will affect how much a loop is transposed when markers with associated keys are used. You can also use this setting to simply transpose a loop without using markers. Lastly, this can be used in conjunction with the regular transposition and tuning settings found in the LCV.

If you find that you are getting clicks and pops in your loop, you might have trimmed the clip on a transient. First, turn off looping on the clip. Then zoom in on the loop to ensure that you have cropped the loop on a zero crossing. In the case of a non-rhythmic sound or a sound that is heavily affected (and contains reverb tails, and so on), you should draw a small fade-in or fade-out on the end of the loop and then use Bounce to Clip before re-looping.

Transient markers are the dotted lines that run vertically in the Loop Construction view. Each marker preserves the timing at its location, so it is important that there are markers where there is important data. There are three ways to edit transient markers. Figure 3.26 shows transient markers in the Loop Construction view.

Based on those two rules, here is a procedure for creating great Groove clips.

1. Double-click the clip to open it in the Loop Construction view.
2. Crop the beginning of the clip so the very beginning is as close to the initial transient as possible (see Figure 3.27). If there is a gap before the first transient, chances are the default slicing is not going to line up with your clip.

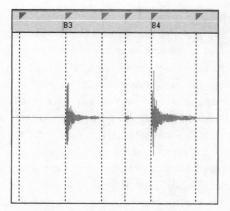

Figure 3.26

Transient markers in the Loop Construction view.

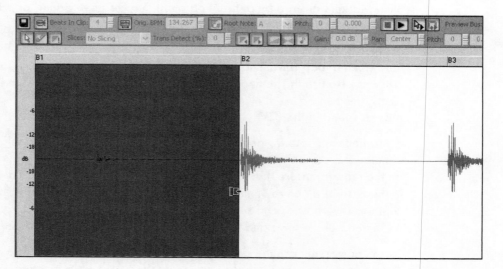

Figure 3.27

Dragging the beginning of the clip to the beginning of the first transient.

3. Crop the end of the clip in the same way, so the clip ends just before the next transient (see Figure 3.28).

4. Click the Enable Looping button to create a Groove clip.

5. If necessary, change the slice value so there are markers at every regular beat, usually quarter or eighth notes work best. You don't want a lot of markers where there is no important material.

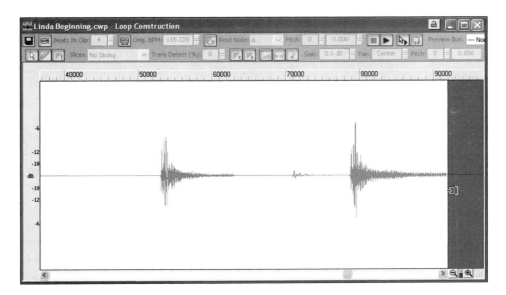

Figure 3.28

Dragging the ending of the clip to the ending of the first transient.

6. Make sure each transient has a marker right at its peak. This preserves the timing of that peak and also preserves the material on the immediate side of the marker. You can drag a marker from elsewhere, if necessary.

7. Make sure any point at which there is a pitch change, like a slurred note or a musical change of interest, has a marker. Again, drag a marker from another point in the clip, if necessary.

8. Listen and adjust the Groove clip markers as necessary.

There are many instances where you might want to create your own loops, whether its for doing a remix at a different tempo, creating a quick "sketch" of a song, or for generating your own loop libraries. The following sections can help you create quality loops like the pros.

Effective Use of Pitch, Pan, and Volume Envelopes

By using the buttons in the LCV, you can show and edit per-slice settings for pitch, pan, or volume on a loop (see Figure 3.29).

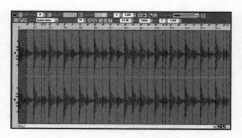

Figure 3.29
Loop Construction view with slice envelopes.

❋ *Pitch* retunes or changes a musical phrase, such as a guitar lick. It can also add variation to static or sampled parts like a repeating conga.

❋ *Volume* creates a chopped effect by turning down every other slice or beat. By using it to a lesser degree, you can replicate a tremolo effect. Sometimes muting the last slice of a loop can create an interesting swing by replicating the way that loops triggered from samplers often sound.

❋ *Panning* on mono drum loops allows you to place components like snares or toms in a stereo field. For special FX, you can create a loop that starts on one side and slowly pans to the other side. You can easily create an auto-panning effect by varying every other beat as well, although this effect can quickly get old.

When you're done, you'll want to save your loop for use in other projects or for collating a library. You can do this directly from the LCV by choosing Save Loop to WAV file or pressing *F*. You might find it faster to simply drag the loop out of the Track view into a folder or onto your desktop. The loop name becomes an amalgamation of the project name, the clip name, and the edit number.

Fixing an Audio Rhythm Track with Quantize

Having the luxury of recording a live drummer can mean a huge improvement to the sound quality and feel of a song. However, there are many scenarios where you might suddenly find that you need to re-work the drums. This can be due to timing inconsistencies or even a production decision to speed up (or slow down) the track. In many modern mixes, live instruments are combined with sequenced or heavily quantized electronic elements, making it essential that man and machine play well together.

Although using Quantize and Groove Quantize seems like the first choice, unlike MIDI tracks where each note is a separate event, each audio take appears as only one event. Therefore, you'll need to break up each hit into separate events by using the Remove Silence command. It might take a little experimentation the first time you use this tool.

1. Select the drum clip to edit. Make sure that it is not a Groove clip (no beveled edges—see Figure 3.30).

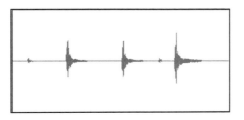

Figure 3.30
A clip ready to be quantized.

2. Zoom in on the waveform vertically and make sure that the audio scale is turned on.

3. Choose Audio > Remove Silence from the Process menu to open the Remove Silence dialog box (see Figure 3.31).

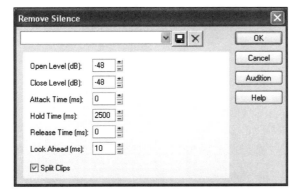

Figure 3.31
The Remove Silence dialog box.

4. In the Remove Silence dialog box, set an Open level that corresponds with the minimum level of the transient for each drum hit. Setting this to high (closer to 0) causes softer hits to be grouped with louder hits like the Kick.

5. Set the Close level a few dB quieter (3 to 6 dB) than the Open level.

6. You will generally want to use a Hold Time of close to 0. Set the Release Time to correspond with the type of drum kit and playing style.

7. Make sure that Split Clips is checked.

8. Before applying the edit, save your settings as a preset. If you find you need to tweak the settings later, you can always save over the existing preset.

Note

You have to click OK to see the results, rather than using the Audition button.

Figure 3.32
Drum track before using Remove Silence.

You will now see that the drum track has been broken up over the length of the file.

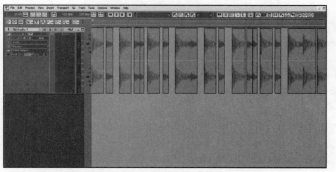

Figure 3.33
Drum track after using Remove Silence.

If you need to tighten or change the timing, you should now use the Quantize or Groove Quantize tool from the Process menu. To preserve some of the human feeling, it is recommended that you try using a strength setting of less than 100%. Depending on this setting, the notes move to somewhere between the original location and the perfectly quantized location.

If you need to fit the drums to musical time (Measure/Beats/Ticks), select the track (or just a verse at a time) and then choose Fit to Time from the Edit menu. Set the format to MBT (you'll see three sets of numbers divided by two colons).

Now set the time to equal the beginning of the measure *after* which you want the drums to stop.

If you need to speed up or slow down the project, assuming the drums are locked to a musical time (see previous two tips), adjusting the tempo will now move the start times of the drum hits accordingly.

Creating Seamless Voice-Overs

Creating voice-overs for commercial work or multimedia presentations (Flash, streaming videos, and so on) can be a challenge, especially when you're used to recording music performances or instruments. Many elements of a vocal performance that are otherwise buried in the mix, become very apparent, and thus much more critical when doing voice-over work.

Removing Breath Sounds

The first step to creating a good voice-over, assuming you've recorded a strong performance from someone with a pleasing voice, is to remove the distraction of breath noises (inhaling, exhaling, sighs, and throat clearing). To do this, use the Audio > Remove Silence command from the Process menu. You'll want to find just the right Open level so that noises before each phrase are removed, but without chopping off the beginning of any words.

Removing noises directly after a group of words is trickier because you'll want to use some Release Time to account for the natural trailing off of a word. Too much release time and you'll also include any noises that follow. If you choose the Split Clips option, it is easy to go back and trim individual phrases to expose or remove time.

Creating Natural Timing

One pitfall to avoid is either spreading out words too far apart or trying to fit them into too short a period of time. By the same token, it is common for readers to pause or stumble momentarily when reading unfamiliar words. Speak the words aloud along with the recording as a gauge. After removing any mistakes, use the Nudge command to make the timing sound as natural as possible. Configure one of the Nudge commands to use only 5-10 milliseconds at a time.

Dealing with Room Tone

After performing all of these edits, you will notice how obvious they are by the sudden absolute silence that marks their location. This is because the subtle background ambience of even the quietest, deadest room has been lost. It also helps, of course, if you are editing the voice-over either in a different location from the original recording or using closed-headphones.

1. Locate the longest section of uninterrupted room tone as possible. You might have to drag out the leading or trailing section of an edited clip to find this.

2. Turn off Snap to Grid by pressing Shift+N.

3. Hold down the Alt key while dragging a marquis around the part of the clip you want to select.

4. Copy the room tone to a new track by holding down the Ctrl key while dragging.

5. Turn on Automatic Crossfades by pressing the X key and copy the room tone wherever there are moments of silence.

6. When you have done this, turn on Show Layers from the Track menu.

7. Drag the room tone onto a layer of the first track; this way, the cross-fades are automatically created so that the transitions aren't noticeable (see Figure 3.34).

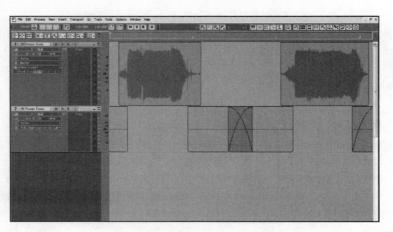

Figure 3.34

Room tone added back to a voice-over.

Thickening Vocal and Instrumental Parts

To get a thicker sound for background vocals or distorted guitars, it is common practice to simply record multiple takes during the session. Sometimes, you will find that only one or two of the takes are really usable, or sometimes you'll realize you need more takes after the fact.

Using the following techniques with only one or two existing takes can certainly create a fuller sound. You can use them by themselves or in combination. Before starting, you need to first clone the track or copy the data to a new track.

Offsetting Timing

Multiple takes, and multiple performers for that matter, are never exactly in time with each other. You can thicken a track by nudging a copy of the track forward or backwards in time. Set the Nudge time to small intervals of milliseconds or even ticks. Moving the cloned track too little results in a phasing effect (sometimes it's cool). Moving it too much results in a flamming or slap back echo sound.

Detuning

Another reality of recording is that seldom are two takes *exactly* in tune. Even if a guitar is carefully calibrated before a take, the playing style of the performer and the exact time that the pick hits the string affect the tuning at any given moment.

To simulate this, you can use SONAR Producer's excellent MPEX 3 pitch algorithm. Selecting one verse or section at a time, choose the Cakewalk Time/Pitch Stretch 2 effect from the Process > Audio Effects menu. Detune by only 5-10 cents at a time until you find a good amount.

EQ and Compression

To emphasize different frequencies and dynamics in each take, try patching a slightly different EQ setting to each track. They should be complementary in nature with some overlap. In addition, although compression is not always necessary, especially on distorted guitar, using subtle compression on one or more of the tracks can help differentiate the two.

Panning

Panning seems like the first port of call for many when trying to create a big track, but too much can reduce the impact of a track. Try not to pan multiple takes more than 20% or 30% to the left or right, unless you're looking for a specific effect. Always check your mixes in mono when using panning as well.

Creating Markers on the Fly

When listening back to a project, you'll often identify problem spots where timing or levels need to be corrected. Pausing the project at each spot to write down the location slows you down. Instead, you can press the F11 key to insert markers on the fly. If you are sitting away from the desk or keyboard at the time, you can even configure this behavior to respond to MIDI information like a note or foot pedal. You set this up in the Key Bindings > Options menu.

Once you're ready to go back to fix the errors, you can jump from marker to marker using the Markers toolbar, Ctrl+Shift+PgUp/PgDown, or again via a custom key binding.

Extracting Timing from an Audio Track to Set Project Tempo

If you have a rhythmic audio track, you can use it to set the project's tempo. With a little tweaking, you can use the Extract Timing dialog box to read the transient information in a track and create a tempo map for your project. To create a tempo map from an audio track, do the following.

1. Maximize the track you want to create a tempo map from and use the Audio Scale ruler to determine the dB level for the transients. Find the smallest beat transient and subtract 3dB from this amount.

2. Select the track you want to create a tempo map from.

3. Choose Process > Audio > Extract Timing from the SONAR menu (see Figure 3.35).

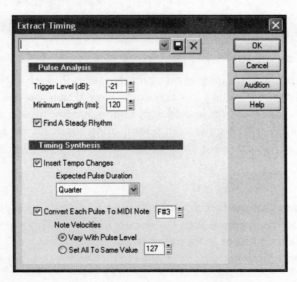

Figure 3.35

The Extract Timing dialog box.

4. In the Extract Timing dialog box, put the value from step 1 into the Trigger Level field.

5. Keep the Minimum Length field at the default value of 120 ms at first.

6. Check the Insert Tempo Changes option. This changes the tempo map to match the timing of the track.

7. Set the Expected Pulse Duration to the number of beats per measure for your transients. For example, if your track is a snare and it hits on the quarter notes, set it to Quarter.

If you get the error message "Required Tempo Exceeds Available Range," increase the Minimum Length field and then try again.

Applying a MIDI Groove to an Audio Track

You can use a MIDI groove to edit an audio clip. Use this procedure to do it:

1. Select a MIDI track, in whole or in part, and copy it to the Clipboard (Ctrl+C).

2. Select the audio track you want to apply the groove to.

3. Choose Audio > Remove Silence from the Process menu.

4. Set an Open level that corresponds with the minimum level of the transient for each drum hit. Setting this to high (closer to 0) causes softer hits to be grouped with louder hits like the Kick.

5. Set the Close level a few dB quieter (3 to 6 dB) than the Open level.

6. You will generally want to use a Hold Time of close to 0. Set the Release Time to correspond with the type of drum kit and playing style.

7. Make sure that Split to Clips is checked.

8. Apply the Groove Quantize command to the selected audio track.

Quantizing a MIDI Track with an Audio Track

Select part of an audio track. Make sure the clip does not have looping enabled. Use a clip that has carefully been cropped and contains a standard number of beats (4, 8, 16, or 32). Also note that this works best with a track with strong transients like a drum or bass track. Now choose Process > Audio > Extract Timing (see Figure 3.36).

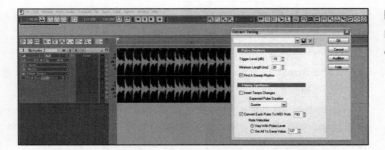

Figure 3.36

Extract Timing dialog box.

❋ Set the Trigger level fairly high at first (closer to 0dB). You can slowly bring this down and press Audition to see the effect.

❋ Set the Hold Time to be fairly short (20 milliseconds or so).

❋ Select Find a Steady Rhythm if it is a fairly busy clip. If the groove is sparse, do not check this.

❋ Insert Tempo Change should not be checked. Convert Each Pulse to MIDI Note should be checked and set to use Vary with Pulse Level.

❋ Press Audition to see an on-screen representation of the extracted rhythm. If it is satisfactory, press OK. The rhythm is now on the Clipboard and will be used when Groove Quantize is selected (see Figure 3.37).

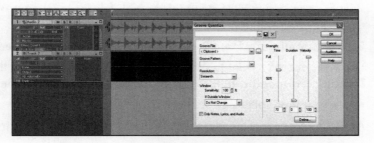

Figure 3.37

Groove Quantize dialog box.

Editing Vocals for Remixing

Many times an artist or record company wants to create a remix to expose a song to club-going audiences. Whether this means turning a ballad into a house track, bumping a slow R&B jam to dancehall, or creating a drum and bass remix of a hip hop track, this typically involves an increase in tempo. Of course, vocals are a main ingredient, allowing listeners to identify the remix with the original song. Even if everything else in the track is new, the vocals represent a hallmark. Here are some tips for reworking vocals to new tempos and styles.

Aligning Phrases to a Beat

If you're changing the swing or groove of the drums, you might find that the vocals don't fall exactly on the beat. You can fix this by using the Quantize or Groove Quantize command. You can also match an existing beat as described in a previous tip.

Some notes:

❀ Sometimes you want to split a single word into several parts before time stretching. For example, you might want to leave the beginning and end of the word unchanged but lengthen (or shorten) the center section. When doing this, be sure to use Automatic Crossfades to make the transitions smooth.

❀ When a singer uses a lot of vibrato, her voice doesn't sound natural if it's stretched too much. Consider shortening the beginning and/or end of the word and simply cropping the middle section.

❀ When working with extreme tempo changes, using the vocals in half-time allows you to make fewer changes.

Lasso Zooming Instantly

Zooming in to take a closer look at a section of your project is as easy as using the Zoom tool, and with the Z key, you can do it instantly. Simply hold down the Z key while left-dragging a rectangle around the section you want to zoom in on, and then release. Figures 3.38 and 3.39 show a lasso zoom selection before and after you release the mouse.

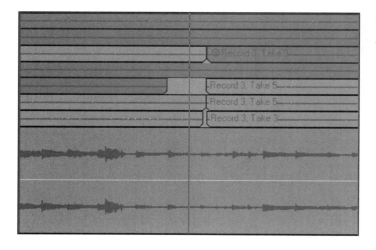

Figure 3.38
A lasso zoom selection.

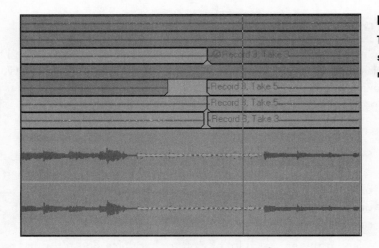

Figure 3.39

The lasso zoom selection after you release the mouse.

Using the Separate Zoom Undo and Redo History

You might have been frustrated when you tried to undo a zoom using Ctrl+Z, because it's not possible. You can, however, undo and redo a zoom using its own undo and redo history. The history allows you to zoom in, make detailed edits, and then zoom out to where you were before you zoomed in. To undo and redo zoom, use the following procedure:

1. Zoom in using the keyboard shortcuts or the vertical or horizontal zoom bars located in the lower right of the Track view (see Figure 3.40).

2. Make whatever edits you want to make (see Figure 3.41).

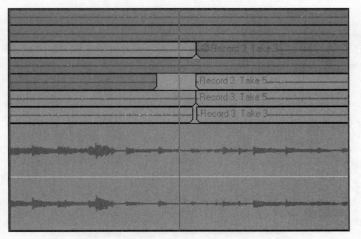

Figure 3.40

Track pane prior to zooming.

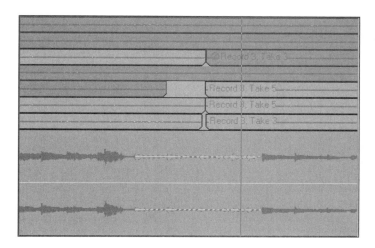

Figure 3.41
Track pane zoomed in.

3. Press the U key to return to the original zoom level (see Figure 3.42).

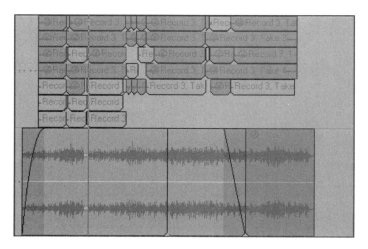

Figure 3.42
Track pane zoomed
out after pressing the
U key.

4. If you want to redo the zoom, hold down the Shift key while pressing U.

4 Mixing and Automation

No two people will ever agree on exactly what makes a good mix good. It is a bit of a mystery even for those who do it every day of their lives. One thing is for sure: Your tools should help you get the sounds you want quickly and easily. This chapter gives you some tips for working quickly and efficiently when mixing your projects.

Using an .ini Variable to Bounce Tracks and Clips Faster

If you are frequently bouncing down to clips or tracks, speeding up the process is an important time-saver. Because mixdown times are affected by your latency settings, you can increase the latency when mixing down to improve performance, but then you need to lower it when recording using input monitoring, which requires very low latency. An easier method is to add a line in the aud.ini file that increases the latency only during mixdown.

Use the following procedure to change the mixdown latency:

1. Open Windows Explorer and navigate to the directory where you installed SONAR.
2. Open aud.ini in Notepad or any text editor.
3. Find the line BounceBufSizeMsec=0.
4. Change the value from 0 to something between 20 and 100. 50 is usually a good number (see Figure 4.1)
5. Save aud.ini.

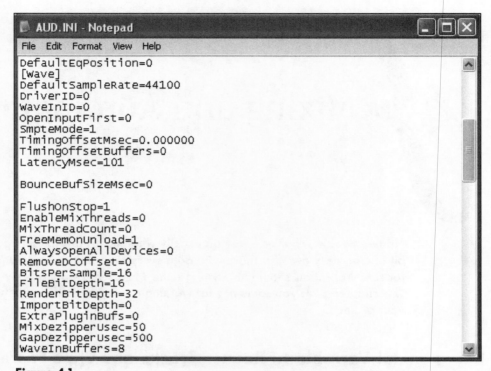

Figure 4.1

The BounceBufSizeMsec line in the aud.ini file.

Conserving CPU with the Freeze Command

If you use a lot of virtual instruments, effects, or both, you might find yourself running out of CPU cycles and getting audio dropouts. Luckily, relief is just a right-click away. The Freeze command is your friend when it comes to getting the most out of your PC. The Freeze command renders a track, creating an audio version of your CPU-hogging synth track. This removes the processing burden from your CPU in exchange for a small increase in your hard drive's throughput. If you need to make changes to the track, simply unfreeze it, make the changes, and refreeze it.

Use the following procedure to Freeze a track.

1. Select the track you want to freeze. If it is a virtual instrument track pair, select the track that contains the virtual instrument.

2. Right-click the track header and choose Freeze > Freeze Track from the menu that appears.

If you are getting less than desirable results using the Freeze command, you might need to adjust the Freeze settings. Use Table 4.1 to troubleshoot any issues that you have.

Table 4.1 Freeze Options and Freeze Troubleshooting

Problem	Solution
Frozen track's reverb or delay is cut off at the end	Open the Freeze Options dialog box shown in Figure 4.2 (right-click a track and choose Freeze > Freeze Options). Increase the number of seconds in the Freeze Tail Duration field.
My synth doesn't seem to want to freeze	Open the Freeze Options dialog box and uncheck the Fast Bounce option. This forces mixdown to happen in real-time, which is required by some synths.
MIDI tracks remain visible when I freeze	Open the Freeze Options dialog box and check Hide MIDI Tracks.

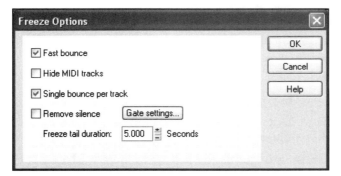

Figure 4.2
Freeze Options dialog box.

Note that you can use the Quick Unfreeze command to temporarily toggle between your rendered audio track and the original track. This is useful when you are using sample-based synths.

Using Grouped Controls to A/B Mixes

With the endless possibilities that modern software affords, it's important to maintain perspective through constant comparisons, or A/Bing between different ent takes, plug-in settings, mixes, or even monitor speakers. Reconfiguring your project's various track settings or routing every time you want to A/B something not only is a pain but also defeats the purpose—by the time you switch from one configuration to the other, you'll forget what the content sounds like.

Fortunately, SONAR includes powerful grouping features that allow you to sync together both similar and dissimilar controls, including volume, pan, and solo controls. The reason this is superior to simply switching the output of a particular bus is that not only can you set different levels for each speaker pair, but you also can remote-control this process via MIDI, which allows you to stand or sit in a certain sweet spot, or away from the computer.

The following sections explain common situations that benefit from A/Bing.

Multiple Sources

This applies to takes, tracks, or even entire mixes. When comparing mixes, it is important that all busses, subgroups, aux (auxiliary), and FX returns for each mix are all routed to a single bus (such as Master, Main, and so on). You can, however, create multiple sends from any track or bus, with each feeding a separate main bus (Mix A, Mix B), so you don't need to recreate all of the busses for each mix.

1. In each mix bus, add the Solo button to the same group.

2. Right-click the grouped control and choose Group Manager from the menu that appears.

3. In the Group Manger dialog box (see Figure 4.3), select the Custom radio button.

4. Select one of the Solo buttons and click the Swap button. The Starting value for one member should equal 0 and the other should equal 1.

5. Press OK.

Soloing one bus (and all of the tracks and busses feeding it) automatically turns off solo on the other bus, in such a way that both busses can never play simultaneously.

You can add mute buttons from additional busses, such as Reverb busses, to the group as well, because soloing a track or bus upstream of a bus does not necessarily prevent other tracks from feeding output through their sends.

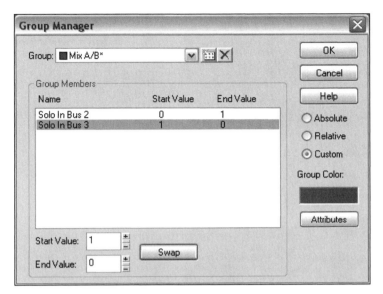

Figure 4.3
Group Manager
dialog box.

Multiple Monitoring Setups

This situation is the opposite of the previous setup to some degree in that it involves routing a single source to multiple locations, but never to all of them simultaneously. For a system with two pairs of monitors, it is a relatively simple affair:

1. Set the main output to your primary monitors.
2. Assign the Track Mute to a new group.
3. Create a Send to the output that feeds an additional pair of monitors.
4. Add the Send Enable to the same group as the mute (see Figure 4.4).
5. Set the Send to Pre-Fader.
6. Go into the Group Manager and swap the values of one control so that they are not on simultaneously.

You can run the subwoofer from a separate Send so you can use it with either of your speaker pairs.

It is recommended that you stop playback and let any tails fade out before switching monitors to avoid pops or potentially speaker-damaging sounds.

Figure 4.4
Grouped Mute buttons and sends.

Offloading Processing to Multiple Workstations

You can take advantage of having multiple computers in order to access additional processing power, to utilize multiple standalone programs that might otherwise conflict, or even to access applications on other platforms such as Macintosh or Linux.

CPU as a Standalone Processor

Another variation involves using a separate computer as a multi-timbral instrument or effects processor. (This has been standard for GigaSampler users for many years.) If you can use a physical MIDI connection to drive the slave computer and route the output to the master computer using a digital connection, the latency should be minimal, with the greatest delay resulting from software monitoring on the main machine, should you be using it. You should run both the master and slave machine at as low a latency as possible.

When triggering instruments hosted in SONAR, you can set up different tracks to respond on different MIDI channels or you can set up layers using the Preset Manager, shown in Figure 4.5, under a track's MIDI Input parameter. This is important because you will want to maximize the number of instruments you drive from one MIDI cable, 16 obviously being the maximum.

For example, when using mono-timbral instrument like PSYN II, you want to confine its input setting to a single channel. Instruments that are multi-timbral (like TTS-1) or that have their own channel assignments can have their MIDI tracks assigned to OMNI. Although it might be initially time consuming, making a preset for each channel on a given port, as well as an omni setting, saves you time if you use this setup on a regular basis.

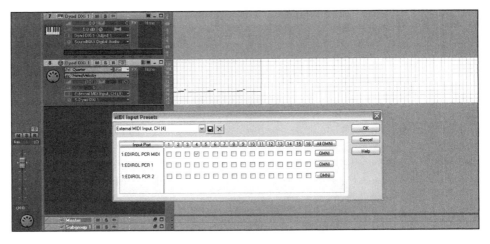

Figure 4.5
MIDI Input Presets dialog box.

Synchronizing Multiple Computers

It is also certainly feasible to slave two (or more) computers together as if you were syncing a tape machine. Again, bussing the output of the other computers into the master computer or a mixer via a digital connection reduces latency.

From within the first computer (the master), go to Options > Project > Sync (see Figure 4.6) and set up the frame rate and the MIDI port that will transmit the timecode.

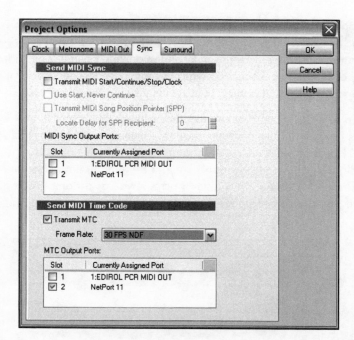

Figure 4.6
Project Options dialog
box's Sync tab with
frame rate and MIDI
port settings.

On any additional computer receiving the timecode that's running SONAR, go
into Options > Global > Time Code, as shown in Figure 4.7, and select Always
Switch Clock Source and Start and Switch Current Clock Source and Start
Playback.

The two computers can be connected via a physical MIDI connection (recommended if they are in close proximity) or via a network MIDI protocol (useful
for machines that are remote or in separate rooms, or if multiple machines
are accessing a single source of timecode). If you have sync issues, first try a
physical MIDI connection to troubleshoot the problem.

If you are having issues with this setup, you can troubleshoot it in a few ways:

❋ If you have sync issues, first try a physical MIDI connection over a virtual
MIDI connection to eliminate variables due to the network.

❋ When running SONAR, check the MIDI monitor icon in the status bar's
notification area. The left-most light indicates MIDI input, the right-most
indicates MIDI output. When sending sync, try muting all MIDI tracks
and checking to make sure the output light still goes on when playing.
For slave computers, check that the left light is active.

❋ For slave machines *not* running SONAR, you can use an application like
MIDI OX to monitor (and analyze) incoming MIDI signals.

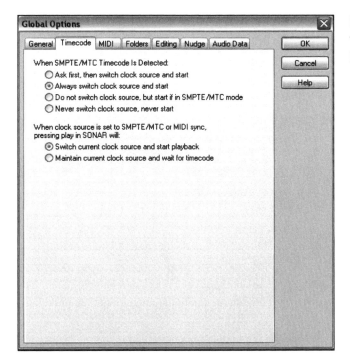

Figure 4.7

The Global Options dialog box's Timecode tab.

Sharing Resources via LAN Using FX:Teleport

The simplest scenario involves using multiple computers to ease the processing load on your computer, without creating multiple projects or complex routings. In this scenario, you can take advantage of several third-party programs that allow you to run plug-ins off of remote computers connected over a network. In any case, you want to use as fast a connection as possible to maximize throughput. Gigabit (1000 MBS) connections via CAT5 cable are the most common, but you can also connect two computers via FireWire (IEEE 1394) and get a bandwidth of 400 or 800 MBS.

All of the utilities listed in this chapter have demo or trial versions available:

The FX Teleport application (http://www.fx-max.com/fxt/) allows you to patch in instruments and effects as you can any normal plug-in; however, the actual processing takes place on a separate machine that streams the audio in and out of your FX insert. When you only have one machine running (no *server*), FX Teleport uses local versions of the plug-ins instead, which is very handy, but also means that you need to install the same plug-ins across multiple machines.

Using FX Teleport:

1. Install all your VSTs on both machines.

2. In SONAR, insert one of the plug-ins on the second machine into an FX bin. The plug-ins on the second machine have (LAN) appended to their names.

3. Begin playback. FX:Teleport begins determining the network latency. You will see it connecting the way it is in Figure 4.8.

Figure 4.8

FX:Teleport connecting.

Tip

One limitation is that the UI for a plug-in run over the LAN will appear on the server, *not* the machine on which you are sequencing. FX:Teleport allows you to load or save presets from the remote machine; you can set up the FX using a local version and then save the preset. Replace the effect with the LAN version (this is how FX Teleport denotes remote effects) and then you can load your preset using the File menu in FX Teleport.

Sharing Resources via LAN Using WormHole

WormHole (see Figure 4.9), available from http://plasq.com/wormhole/ is a clever little plug-in that creates virtual audio outputs that you can route out of or into SONAR. These virtual outputs can be routed to another instance of WormHole, either locally or across a network to bridge multiple machines. Because WormHole is cross-platform, it's a great way to bridge the ubiquitous Mac/Windows gap.

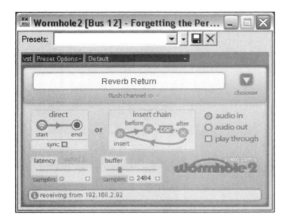

Figure 4.9

WormHole.

To use WormHole to route the output of one computer running SONAR into another, do the following:

1. Open the main output bus on the source computer and choose WormHole 2 from the VST effects menu.
2. Type in a new channel name.
3. Uncheck Play Through.
4. Select the Direct Start option on the left.
5. On the receiving computer, create a new track and insert WormHole 2 on the insert.
6. From the drop-down menu, you should be able to select the channel name you entered. WormHole2 will show the IP address of the machine sending the audio.
7. Adjust the buffer setting on the receiving machine to achieve a good balance of sound quality and latency. Lower is better.
8. Adjust the latency slider on the sending machine to change the amount of latency reported to SONAR so that SONAR's engine may compensate for it.

9. While playing you should see the appropriate input and output lights turn yellow to indicate activity.

Note

If WormHole gives the message "the host is not feeding audio to WormHole2," then you should arm or activate input monitoring on that track.

To use WormHole to process the tracks from one machine, using effects on a second machine, do the following:

1. On the machine that will host the effects, place an instance of WormHole2 in an insert.
2. Type in a channel name, such as Insert Test.
3. Choose the option labeled Insert Chain Before.
4. Insert the effect or effects you wish to use for processing.
5. Add another instance of WormHole2 immediately after this effect and select the same channel name from the drop-down menu. The After button should be selected (in blue).
6. Again, you may need to arm or input monitor the track if WormHole2 reports no audio received.
7. On the machine from which you wish to send the unprocessed audio, insert WormHole2 on a track or bus.
8. Select the channel name from the bottom half of the channel drop-down menu.
9. Press play and you will now hear the processed audio.

See Figure 4.10 for an example of Wormhole as an insert.

Figure 4.10

Wormhole as an insert.

Sharing Resources via LAN using MIDIoverLAN CP

MIDIoverLAN CP, available at http://www.musiclab.com/products/rpl_info.htm, allows you to share Virtual MIDI ports over a network between Mac and PC, as shown in Figure 4.11. These ports can trigger instruments remotely or synchronize two machines (although latency might require that you set an offset on one of the machines).

In use, MIDIoverLAN CP works like any other MIDI ports when used within SONAR. The most important part is the initial setup, however.

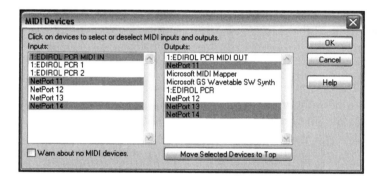

Figure 4.11

Selecting MIDIoverLAN ports in the MIDI Devices dialog box.

Points to remember:

* Each port can be local (for connecting multiple apps on one machine), can send to another IP address, or can receive from another IP.

* You can configure ports to respond to data sent on remote ports of a specific number. Forcing ports of only the same number to communicate on multiple machines can help you keep organized.

* MIDIoverLAN includes a MIDI Monitor that you access by double-clicking the MIDIoverLAN icon in the system tray.

* To determine the IP of any given machine, go to Start > Control Panel > Network Connections and double-click your active connection. Go to the Support tab to see your IP address.

Accessing External Processors via Universal Bus Architecture

Although software has made incredible strides in terms of sound quality and usability, many people still find themselves in situations where they want to use a tried-and-true favorite piece of hardware—whether it be a famed Lexicon reverb, crusty Space Echo, or the grit of an old tube preamp. This tip shows you how to extend the flexibility of software to include hardware processors as well.

You can integrate hardware into SONAR in several ways. The most obvious way is to use hardware to process what you are recording into the computer. However, this method does not allow for the processing of multiple channels (unless you are also using a hardware mixer) and is a destructive process, thus making it impossible to change the quality or nature of the sound later.

A much better approach is to patch external gear from the outputs of the computer, allowing you to dynamically assign any number of tracks to the hardware output and monitor, or even re-record the results from an additional track. Although the setup might seem a bit complicated, there is no limit to the possibilities afforded by the Universal Bus Architecture in SONAR. It allows unlimited tracks and busses, infinite numbers of gain stages, and monitoring at every level. Once you've created one of these monstrous setups, you can save it as a Track Preset for later use, provided you don't change the way that your hardware is patched.

To begin, you need to have enough physical connections on your audio inter-face to allow a dedicated connection to a piece of external gear. Preferably, you should use a SPDIF or Optical connection because the lack of A/D and D/A conversion will reduce latency. This also requires your external processor to have SPDIF or Optical I/O.

Follow this procedure for using external processors as an aux bus:

1. Create a bus in SONAR and name it accordingly (*Reverb Tank*, for example—see Figure 4.12).

Figure 4.12

Reverb Tank bus.

2. Assign the bus output to the outputs connected to your hardware.

3. Create and assign sends on any tracks you want to access the external effect (see Figure 4.13).

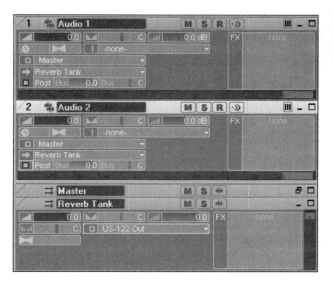

Figure 4.13

Tracks with sends to the Reverb Tank bus.

4. Create a new audio track and call it *Reverb Tank Return*. Set its inputs to the inputs connected to the hardware output (see Figure 4.14).

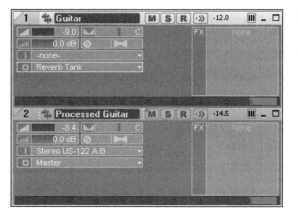

Figure 4.14

Track with inputs from outboard reverb processor.

5. Route the *Return* track directly to your main output bus.

6. Activate input monitoring on the track, as shown in Figure 4.15.

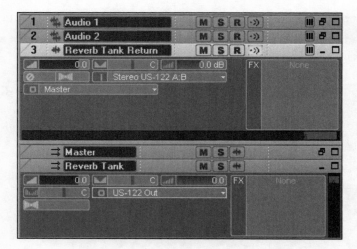

Figure 4.15
External processing.

Keep in mind that you can easily overload the external processor without seeing any obvious peaking in SONAR because the hardware most likely has its own input gain stage.

Use this procedure to use external processors non-destructively on an insert:

1. Using a new or pre-recorded track, set the output to go directly to the audio output(s) connected to your hardware. Many times audio hardware is monophonic, so you might want to hard-pan the track to the appropriate channel.

2. For now, disable any sends on the track. Mixing sends from the dry track with the processed track can lead to interesting results, however.

3. Create a new audio track, immediately below the original track, and label it accordingly (see Figure 4.16). Set the input to the output of the processor. Its output can go directly to any bus you want, in addition to using any aux sends. *Make sure that you are not routing any of the outputs back into the hardware unit!*

4. If recording a new track, activate software monitoring on the original (dry) track. If not, leave this off.

5. Mute the processed track and turn on input monitoring.

6. On playing, you should see signal on both the original track and the processed track. Adjust your external processor until the return level is satisfactory.

7. Unmute the processed track.

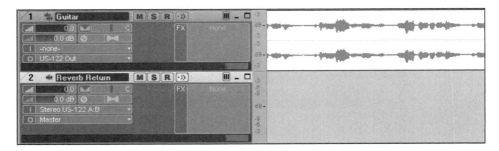

Figure 4.16

Original track with processed return track beneath.

In this example, when recording a new track, perceived latency is twice what it normally is because you are monitoring the signal twice. If you can reduce your soundcard latency to 3 or 4 ms, this might prove acceptable. Otherwise, you can choose to split the output of the external processor, monitoring directly from an output while recording with the other.

Automating Smooth Crossfades Between Multiple Tracks

SONAR offers an automatic crossfade; however, you are limited to preset curves and the clips must be on the same track. Envelopes give a much higher level of control but they take longer to draw and, when trying to manage envelopes on two tracks, it becomes more time consuming. There are also situations where you might want to adjust the balance between two tracks (a direct signal and mic signal, for example) without exceeding a certain sound level (you want to make one or more tracks quieter as you boost another track). A convenient way to create quick crossfades in real-time, via mouse or MIDI, is to use grouping.

1. Right-click the volume control for the first track (or bus) and assign it to an unused group.
2. Right-click the second volume control and do the same.
3. Right-click again and go into the Group Manager. Choose Custom (see Figure 4.17).
4. Swap the ranges of one of the controllers so that it is opposite of the other, as shown in Figure 4.18. You can limit the ranges here as well. Click OK.

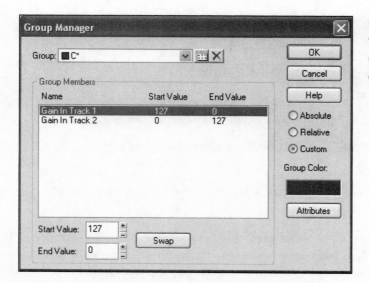

Figure 4.17

The Custom option in the Group Manager dialog box.

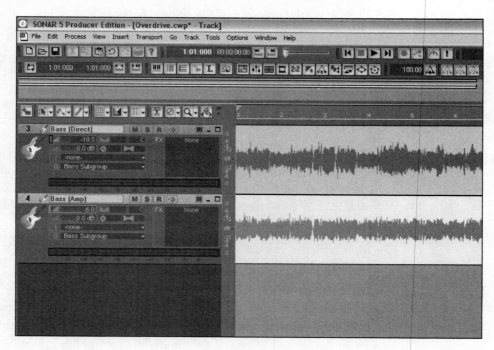

Figure 4.18

Volume of two tracks grouped inversely.

You are now set up to manually balance multiple tracks by simply adjusting a single fader. To record automation:

1. Arm both widgets for automation by right-clicking the volume slider in each track and selecting Arm for Automation.

2. Record automation and you will see two complementary automation curves (see Figure 4.19).

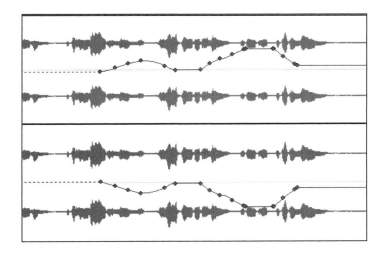

Figure 4.19

Two automation curves after recording automation on inversely grouped volume controls.

3. If you want to record automation via MIDI, set up remote control for one of the widgets.

You can also use this technique with good success using pan controls.

Multiband and Parallel Processing Techniques

A technique that you can use for both creative and more surgical processing is multi-band processing. Common in dynamics plug-ins, the method translates well to any type of effect, whether delay-, dynamics-, or modulation-based. This example assumes you are running an entire mix, but you can easily apply the technique to individual tracks.

1. Create four new busses. Label them Final, Low, Mid, and High.

2. Activate the per-channel EQ on each bus (or load your favorite provided it has adequate control) and set them up as follows:

❄ Final—Send this bus to your main outputs.

❄ Low—Use Low-Pass or High-Shelf filtering with an upper range of between 250 and 300 Hz. Route the output to the Final bus.

❄ Mid—Use a Band-Pass Filter (or a combination of Low and High Pass). The low range should be between 250 and 300 Hz and the upper range should be between 2000 and 3000 Hz. Route the output to the Final bus.

❄ High—Use a High-Pass or Low-Shelf Filter with the bottom range set to between 2000 and 3000 Hz. Route the output to the Final bus.

3. Mute or disable the main output from your master bus. Create three sends and route them to each of the new busses. Activate them and set the levels. They will all be routed back to the new final bus.

4. Because the default EQ in SONAR is not capable of a very extreme sloping (see Figure 4.20), you might need to experiment with the frequency and cross-over the various bands. The goal is to avoid creating a gap in the frequency range while also avoiding sending the same frequency through multiple bands, which can create bumps in the spectrum or phasing issues. Before applying FX, you should get the mix sounding comparable to how it sounded through a single bus.

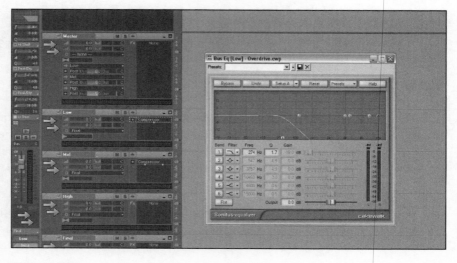

Figure 4.20

Multiband EQ.

* Try reducing the stereo image of the low-frequency to eliminate muddiness or to make the mix more suitable for playback over club PA systems.

* The high frequencies will suffer the most noticeably from over-compression, so it is best to avoid most dynamics processing here. You will notice effects like reverb easily on the higher frequencies, however.

* Adjusting the output volume of each bus will greatly affect the timbre of the resulting track, acting like an EQ. You should always make adjustments more subtle than you think they should be at the time.

* Try using effects like delay, tremolo, or distortion on just the mid or high bands when processing individual tracks to create an interesting sound without losing the drive or punch.

* Overcompressing the low or mid band and leaving the other bands untouched can provide good results when recombined.

Using Vertical Track Zoom for More Precise Automation Node Editing

If you find you are having trouble making precise edits to automation nodes in the Track view, you can easily increase the node resolution by zooming in on a track. See Figures 4.21 and 4.22.

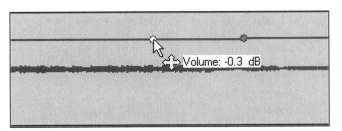

Figure 4.21

Track prior to zooming with a resolution of .3 dB.

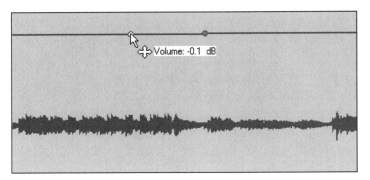

Figure 4.22

Track after zooming with a resolution of .1 dB.

Using Your MIDI Controller as a Control Surface

In the last few years, control surfaces have become more and more common in many home studios. For those who started off on a four-track or on an audio console, adding a tactile element to your mixing makes the process seem more natural. It might not be necessary for those who have a MIDI controller to make the additional investment in a control surface because SONAR gives you the capability to map MIDI controls to application commands. Some newer controllers have added faders and knobs, giving you additional control over SONAR.

There are two methods for controlling SONAR using your MIDI controller. Even if your controller has assignable knobs and sliders, you can use certain musical keys on your controller to execute commands or enter Shift mode, which toggles your keyboard from a musical controller to a control surface, allowing you to assign as many keys as you want to commands in SONAR.

Using Key Bindings with Your Control Surface

Use the following procedure to assign keys on your controller to commands in SONAR:

1. Choose Options > Key Bindings from the SONAR menu (see Figure 4.23).

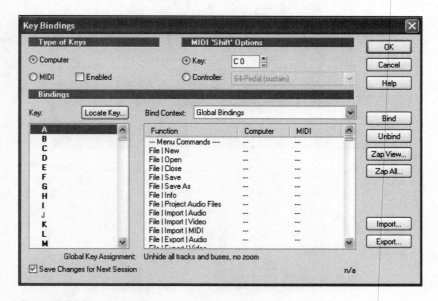

Figure 4.23
The Key Bindings dialog box.

2. In the Type of Keys section, click the MIDI radio button.

3. In the Bindings section, select a key on the left side and choose the command you want to map it to on the right side.

4. Click the Bind button.

5. In the MIDI Shift Options section, select either the Key or Controller radio button. Use the Key setting if you want to use a key on your controller. Use the Controller setting if you want to use a widget.

6. If you are using the Key option, set the key setting to the key on your controller you want to use. Often a good choice is a seldom if ever used key, such as C10 (see Figure 4.24).

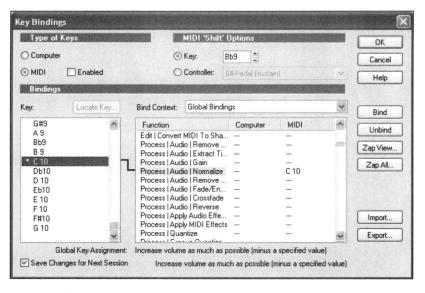

Figure 4.24

A MIDI keyboard note assigned to a command in the Key Bindings dialog box.

7. If you are using the Controller option, set the Controller setting to a MIDI setting assigned to one of your widget controls.

8. Click OK.

On your controller, press the Shift key or controller and then use any of the key bindings you have assigned to execute commands.

Mapping Controls to Commands Using a Generic Control Surface

Use the following procedure to assign your controller to a generic control surface in SONAR:

1. Choose Options > Control Surfaces from the SONAR menu.
2. Click the Add New Control Surface button in the Control Surfaces dialog box (see Figure 4.25).

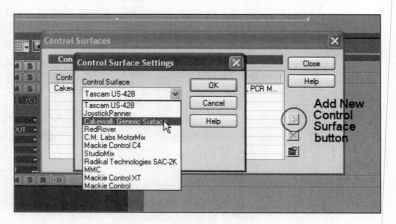

Figure 4.25

Add New Control Surface button.

3. In the Control Surface Settings dialog box, set the Input and Output port to the control you are using. Click OK.
4. Close the Control Surfaces Settings dialog box.

Use the following procedure to map commands to your controller's widgets to the generic control surface:

1. Choose Tools > Cakewalk Generic Surface from the SONAR menu. You will see the dialog box in Figure 4.26.
2. Assign parameters to the widgets on your controller.
3. For controller-specific information, consult your controller's documentation.

Figure 4.26

Generic Control Surface dialog box.

Using an .ini Variable to Change
Pre-Fader Behavior when Muting a Track

Some people are thrown off when they can still hear their muted tracks. The reason, of course, is that their pre-fader sends are still routed to a bus. This is as it should be, but not the way it has to be. You can change this behavior by adding a line in your aud.ini file.

To force your pre-fader sends to mute when the track is muted, do the following:

1. Open Windows Explorer and navigate to the directory where you installed SONAR.
2. Open aud.ini in Notepad or any text editor.
3. Add the line `LinkPFSendMute=1` (see Figure 4.27).

Figure 4.27

The `LinkPFSendMute` line in the aud.ini file.

4. To revert to the old behavior, simply change the value to 0 (zero).
5. Save aud.ini.

Using a Free Utility to Align Delayed Audio Signals with Other Tracks

If you have a DirectX plug-in that has a high latency, you can use a free utility called SampleSlide (available at http://www.analog-x.com) to line up the problem track with the rest of your tracks. Use the following procedure to do so.

1. Create a bus for your tracks that do not have a latency problem and assign those tracks to that bus.

2. Insert SampleSlide (download it from http://www.analog-x.com) in the bus's FX bin. You will see the interface shown in Figure 4.28.

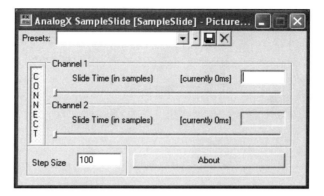

Figure 4.28

SampleSlide interface.

3. Listen to your project and adjust the slider settings in SampleSlide so your audio matches up.

Finding the Highest Volume Peak in a Track

It can be frustrating trying to find the one or two quick, high transients in a project, but with SONAR 5's new *peak markers,* it takes you no time at all, giving you a quick look at the parts you might want to tame so you don't clip when raising the gain on the track.

To find the peak volume of a track:

1. If you have not already done so, turn on the Show Track Peak Markers option (see Figure 4.29) from the Show/Hide All Meters drop-down menu.

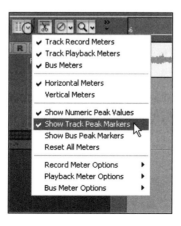

Figure 4.29

Show Track Peak Markers option.

2. Play your project. Each time a track's volume exceeds the previous peak, the peak marker is updated at the top of the clip (see Figure 4.30).

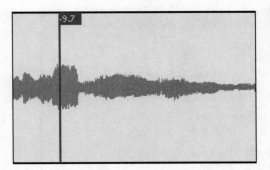

Figure 4.30

A peak marker showing the highest volume on the track.

3. Once you have played the entire track, right-click the peak volume display on the track header and choose Go to Peak. This moves the now time to the peak marker (see Figure 4.31).

Figure 4.31

The Go to Peak command.

Cycling through Markers on the Time Ruler

A complex project can have dozens of markers on the time ruler. Often these markers end up stacked on top of each other. If you attempt to move one marker, you might end up moving a different one. Here is a little trick you can use to select the right marker before dragging it to a new location.

1. Move your cursor over the marker stack, and then click it and hold.

2. Press the Tab key, as shown in Figure 4.32. Each time you press Tab, a new letter appears. The letters represent the type of marker in the stack. Once you have found the right letter (see Table 4.2), drag the marker to its new location.

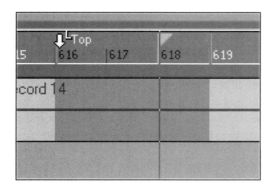

Figure 4.32

Cycling through markers
using the Tab key.

Table 4.2 Tab Key Letters and What They Represent

Letter	Type of Marker
L	Loop marker
P	Punch marker
T	Now time marker
M	Marker

Side-Chaining Compressors and Gates

One of the more common mixing techniques that SONAR does not address is side-chaining and keying of compressors and gates. However, there are several ways around this issue, using both Cakewalk and free third-party plug-ins.

The venerable FX1 Dynamics Processing Suite (see Figure 4.33) included with SONAR is still a very comprehensive solution for compression, expansion, and gating. The plug-ins are two channel affairs, meaning that they can operate in stereo or side-chain mode. When Stereo Interaction switches to side-chain, the left signal will drive the processor, whereas the right side will be the signal passed through the effect.

The easiest way to use this plug-in is to patch it to a new bus and route both the track to be processed and the key track to this bus. You'll also want to hard-pan the outputs of each track—keying track to the left channel, and the other to the right channel. The output of the plug-in is monophonic but it is applied to both channels.

You can still pass a stereo signal by using two instances of the plug-in, each on its own bus. Create an additional send from the key signal track and send it to the second bus, again hard-panning the send to the left. Although the signal track will run through the right channel of the processor, you're actually processing the left channel of the original signal. To do this you need to insert another bus between the original track and the bus with the dynamics processor on it. This is because panning a stereo signal simply changes the mix of the two channels. Short of summing to mono, you can't force one channel to play through the other. The idea is that you use a send from the original track, hard-panned *right* to an intermediate bus, which you force to *mono*, and then hard-pan to the *left* and out to the dynamic processing bus.

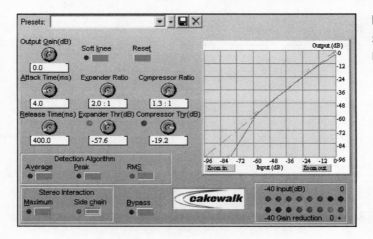

Figure 4.33
SONAR's Dynamic Processor.

It should also be noted that you don't *have* to use a separate signal for keying the compressor or gate. You can, for example, split up a track and run one chain through an EQ before side-chaining the other side; in this way, you can remove sibilance and accomplish many other things.

For many common applications like voice-over work or for creating stuttering pads and the like, FX1 is a very easy and useful tool.

Another way that you can easily process stereo tracks with dynamics while using side-chaining, albeit with a bit less control, is to use the Sonitus SurroundComp, shown in Figure 4.34. Designed for multi-channel use, it can easily be used for side-chaining even if you aren't working with a surround project.

Figure 4.34
Sonitus Surround
Compressor.

1. Go to Options > Project > Surround and set the Downmixing level of the Surround Channels to –INF (see Figure 4.35).

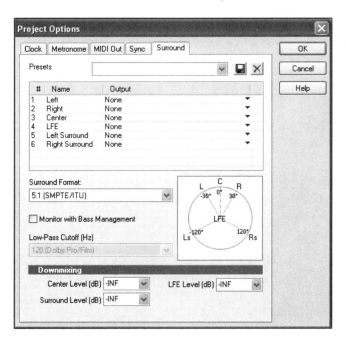

Figure 4.35
All surround downmixing settings set to -INF in the Surround tab of the Project Options dialog box.

2. Send the output of the track you want to process to a new *surround* bus. Make sure it is panned to the front (see Figure 4.36).

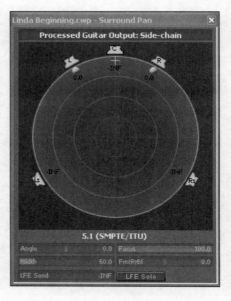

Figure 4.36

Track panned to front speakers only.

3. Send the output of the track you want to side-chain with to the same surround bus. Now open the surround panner and route the signal to the rear speakers only (see Figure 4.37).

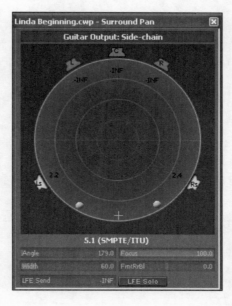

Figure 4.37

Track panned to rear speakers only.

4. Send the output of the surround bus to your main *stereo* bus.

5. Insert the Sonitus SurroundComp on the surround bus. Make sure that the front and rear speakers are in the same group (see Figure 4.38).

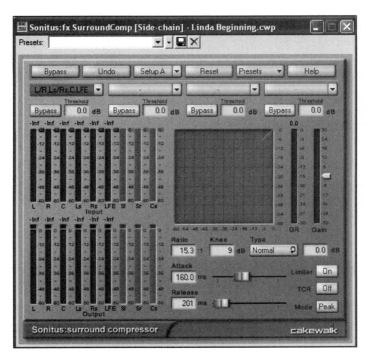

Figure 4.38

The Sonitus:fx Surround Compressor.

6. You can set the compression mode to Peak or Sum, the latter being more subtle. You can start with Peak mode.

7. Adjust the threshold by moving the triangular sliders up and down. All channels in the group are affected simultaneously. As you bring the threshold down, you should hear the side-chaining become more obvious.

8. In Peak mode, the loudest signal will effectively trigger the compressor. With downmixing turned off and the surround bus being routed to a stereo track, you should not hear the side-chaining signal. You can therefore adjust the level of that track to increase or reduce the level triggering the compressor.

9. If you want to still use the key signal in your mix (it might be your kick drum for example), simply use a send from the track instead of the main out. Be sure to use the same routing and pan settings, as described.

Using Digital Peak Meter for Side-Chaining

The preceding solutions deal with effective side-chaining when compressing or gating a track. You can actually side-chain a filter, delay, or just about any other type of compressor, by using features of the *Digital Peak Meter*, shown in Figure 4.39, which can be obtained for free from http://software.bluecatonline.org/ DPeakMeter.htm.

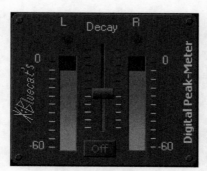

Figure 4.39
Bluecat's Digital Peak Meter.

Insert the plug-in on the track you want to use as the side-chain source and be sure to set the appropriate channel mode (mono or stereo). Right-click the effects bin and choose Arm Parameter and then choose the Envelope Out parameter. When you choose Record Automation, SONAR will record an envelope that follows the output level of the track, which will look like Figure 4.40. When done, this envelope can be reassigned to any track or effects parameter (Volume, Pan, or Filter Hz) and copied and pasted to any number of tracks.

✴ To adjust the release time, move the Decay slider in the plug-in. The plug-in's own meter will show you real-time results.

✴ You can also delay or pre-delay the side-chaining by simply sliding the envelope forward or backward.

While the limitation of this method is that it is obviously not a real-time affair, it offers tons of flexibility in what you can achieve. For example, you might control delay time or mix level according to track volume.

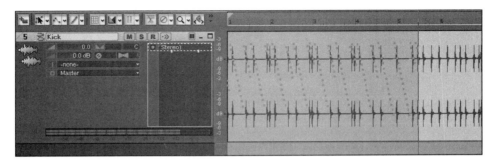

Figure 4.40

Envelopes in the Track pane.

Toggling Quickly Between Alternative Versions Using Track Folders

Quickly toggling from one version of a mix to another can save you minutes that you can put to better use working on the next project. Track folders are a great way to organize your project; they give you a way to move from one mix to the next in no time at all.

1. Create as many folder tracks as you have mixes. In this example, there are just two.

2. Place all the tracks exclusive to each mix in their respective track folders.

3. Label each track folder descriptively. In this example, the drums in Figure 4.41 are played with sticks on one mix and with brushes on the second mix, so they are labeled Drums Brushes and Drums Sticks.

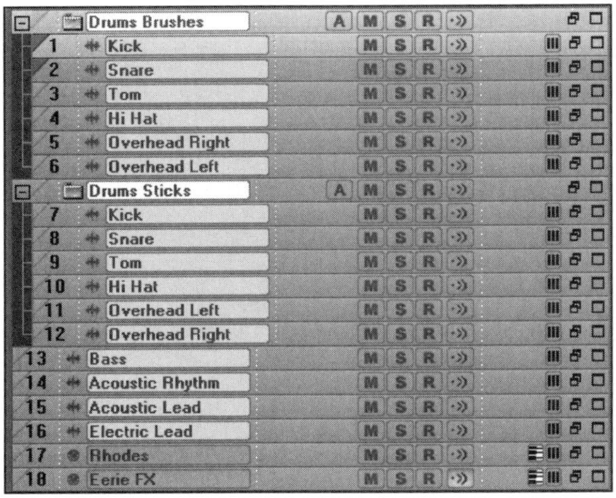

Figure 4.41

Track folders containing two different drum takes.

4. Mute one track folder and play your project to hear a mix, as shown in Figure 4.42.

5. Unmute the first track folder and mute the second to hear the second mix.

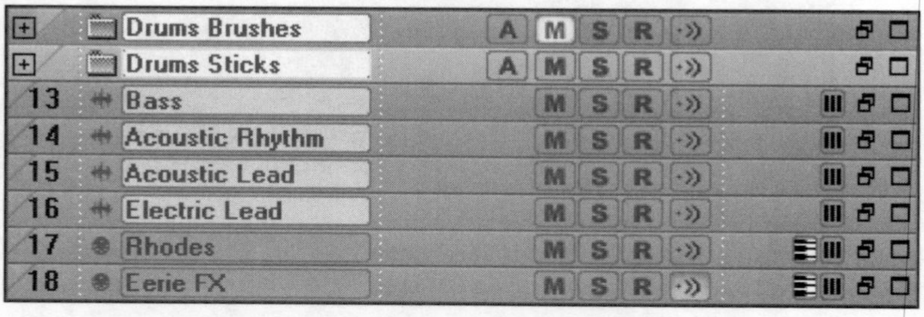

Figure 4.42
Track folders minimized with the first track muted.

Quickly Grouping Controls without Using Control Groups

If you find yourself using grouping a lot in SONAR, but wish it was faster, SONAR 5 has introduced a feature for you: *quick grouping*. Now you can create temporary groups of like controls as quickly as selecting the tracks you want to modify.

To use quick grouping:

1. Click the triangle in the upper-left corner of one of the tracks you want to select. The triangle turns blue when it's selected.

2. Select additional tracks by dragging them if they are contiguous or by holding down the Ctrl key and selecting them.

3. Adjust the parameter you want to change in each track (pan, volume, and so on). For example, in Figure 4.43, the volume is being adjusted.

4. Click anywhere to deselect the tracks.

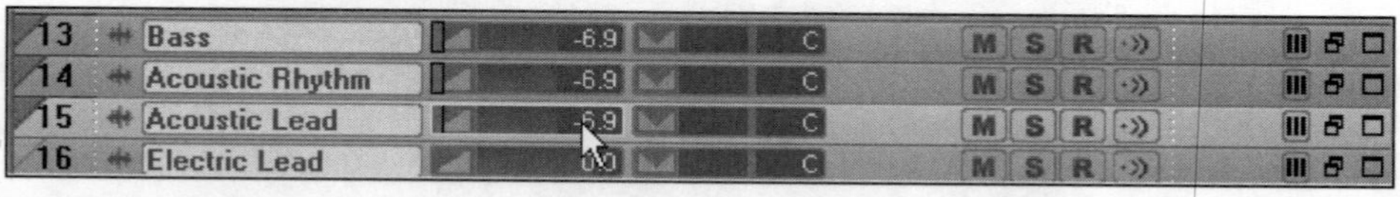

Figure 4.43
Changing the volume of three quick-grouped tracks.

Saving a Bus as the Default in a Track Template

Track templates are very powerful and easy to use. One of the ways they save you time is by allowing you to add a track and a bus at the same time. Most of us like to use the same overall structure when we are working, so when it's time to add lead vocals, you probably also want to add a bus to route it through.

First you create a track template:

1. Customize a track including its name, FX, bus output, and so on.
2. Right-click the track and choose Save as Track Template.
3. In the Export Track Template dialog box, enter a name for your track template.
4. Click Save.

Start a new project, using the Normal template, like I do in Figure 4.44. Now, you add a track based on the track template and get the bus it is routed to.

1. Right-click anywhere in the Track pane.
2. Choose Insert Track from Track Template from the menu that appears.
3. Select the Track Template you just saved. Your project should look like the one in Figure 4.45.

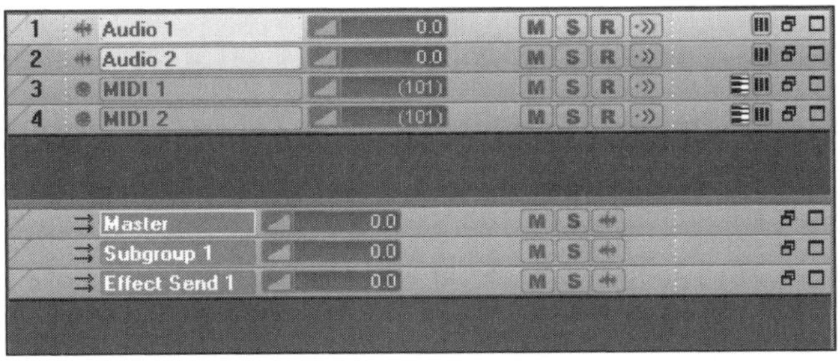

Figure 4.44

New project before track template inserted.

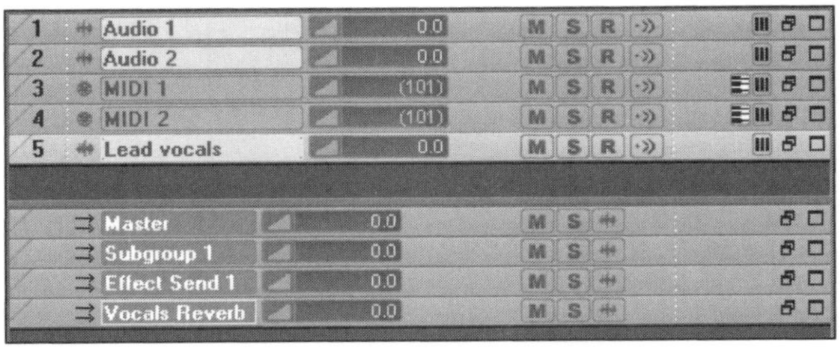

Figure 4.45

New project after track template inserted; note the addition of the track template's bus.

Instantly Adding Nodes to the Beginning and End of an Envelope

If you need to add two nodes to an envelope, there is a very quick way to do this based on the current selection.

1. Select a range in the time ruler on the boundaries of where you want the nodes placed.
2. Right-click the envelope and choose Add Nodes at Selection. See Figure 4.46.

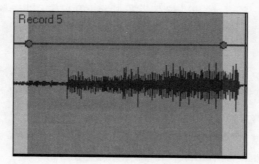

Figure 4.46

Nodes created at the beginning and the end of a time ruler selection.

Fixing Stray Notes Using Clip Effects and EQ

A stray buzzing note in an otherwise perfect guitar solo can make you pull your hair out. Before you call up the guitar player for another session, however, you can take advantage of SONAR 5's new clip-based effects and EQ to reduce the offending sound to the point where it disappears in the mix.

1. Use the Split tool to create a clip consisting of just the place where the bad notes are.
2. Right-click the clip you just created and choose Insert Effect > Audio > Sonitus:fx > Equalizer, as shown in Figure 4.47.

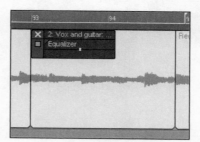

Figure 4.47

Clip with Sonitus:fx Equalizer.

3. Loop playback of just the clip you are trying to fix.

4. Using one of the bands in the Sonitus:fx EQ, change the Q setting to 24 and raise the level to about 10 to 12dB while sweeping the frequency.

5. When you hear the bad notes amplified, lower the dB level to -10dB.

6. You might need to tweak the Q setting and the frequency.

5 } Working with MIDI

MIDI is an old technology, but despite the years, rather than being obsolete, its flexibility has made it a central part of music-making for both professionals and hobbyists alike. SONAR has always been one of the best MIDI sequencers on the market, and SONAR 5's new features only add to that reputation. With software synthesizers and samplers, MIDI is now as hot as ever. The tips in the chapter help you get more out of your MIDI music experience.

Modifying Instrument Definitions to Appear at the Top of the List

If you have a lot of instrument definitions, it can be hard to find the exact one you want to use. More than likely, you use a few of them more often than the others. You can put those instrument definitions at the top of the list by adding a special character, like an underscore. With your preferred instrument definitions at the top of the Assign Instruments dialog box, it becomes much easier to find and select the instrument definition you want. To move an instrument definition to the top of the list:

1. Choose Options > Instruments from the SONAR menu. The Assign Instruments dialog box appears (see Figure 5.1).
2. Click the Define button to open the Define Instruments and Names dialog box.
3. Right-click on an instrument definition you use often and choose Edit from the menu that appears.
4. Add an underscore to the beginning of the instrument definition's name and press Enter (see Figure 5.2).

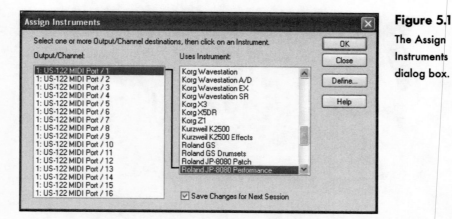

Figure 5.1

The Assign Instruments dialog box.

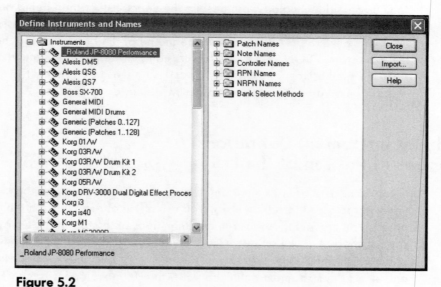

Figure 5.2

An instrument definition with its name edited to include an underscore at the beginning.

5. Click Close. The instrument definitions appear at the top of the list in the Assign Instruments dialog box (see Figure 5.3).

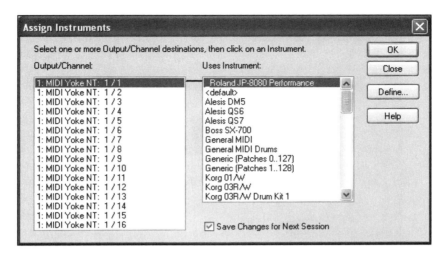

Figure 5.3
The instrument definition with its name at the top of the list.

Improving Performance of MFX Plug-ins

If you are unhappy with the performance of your MFX plug-ins, perhaps because there is a delay between input and processing, this might be caused by too much of a buffer between input and execution. This is needed for quantize or to perform other operations that require a look-ahead, but can be problematic when using MFX plug-ins. There is an .ini variable you can add to the ttsseq.ini file that might improve it. This new ttsseq.ini variable defines how much extra MIDI data is sent to MFX plug-ins. Lower values mean MFX plug-ins can work in real-time. To edit this variable, use the following procedure:

1. Exit SONAR if it is running.
2. Navigate to where you installed SONAR 5.
3. In the SONAR 5 folder, open the ttsseq.ini file using Notepad or any text editor.
4. Add the following line to the section [OPTIONS]:

   MfxLookAhead=480

   See Figure 5.4 for how this looks in ttsseq.ini.
5. Save the ttsseq.ini file.

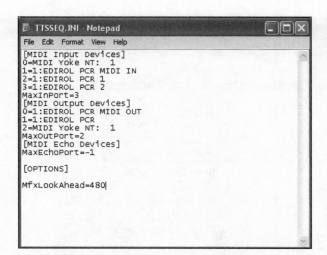

Figure 5.4

The MfxLookAhead
line in ttsseq.ini.

Editing MIDI Notes in the Track View

New with SONAR 5 is the capability to edit MIDI in the Track view. In every
MIDI track you can toggle between displaying MIDI data as clips or notes. If a
track is assigned to a drum map, notes appear as drum notes. Once enabled,
you can edit MIDI just as you do in the Piano Roll view. Follow these steps to
get going:

1. Choose View > Toolbars and check Inline Piano Roll in the Toolbar dialog
   box to display the Inline Piano Roll toolbar (see Figure 5.5).

Figure 5.5

The Inline Piano Roll toolbar.

2. Click the PRV Mode button in the MIDI track's header. The PRV Mode
   button adds several MIDI note menus to the track and turns the track
   itself into a piano roll (MIDI note grid). See Figure 5.6.

3. Select a tool in the Inline Piano Roll toolbar and edit your MIDI track.

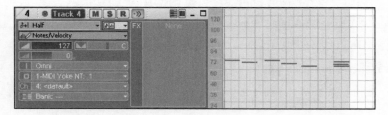

Figure 5.6

A track with the
PRV Mode button
enabled.

Using the MIDI Scale in the Track View

The new PRV Mode in the Track view allows you to do most of your work in one view. To get the most out of the PRV Mode, you need to know how to use the MIDI Scale. Table 5.1 explains how to zoom in and out and preview notes in the MIDI Scale.

Table 5.1 Using the MIDI Scale

To Do This	Do This
Zoom in	Click on the MIDI Scale and drag up.
Zoom out	Click on the MIDI Scale and drag down.
Scroll up	Right-click on the MIDI Scale and drag up.
Scroll down	Right-click on the MIDI Scale and drag down.
Scale the track so that all of the contents fit in the track	Right-click on the MIDI Scale and choose Fit Content.
Audition a note	Click on the note in the MIDI Scale.

Figure 5.7 shows what the cursor looks like as you drag on the MIDI Scale.

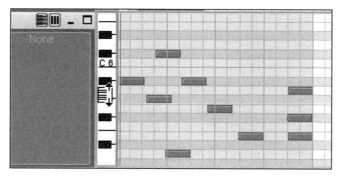

Figure 5.7

The MIDI Scale cursor.

Using the Fretboard Pane to Transcribe MIDI Files into Guitar TAB

MIDI files, often available for free on the Internet, are great tools for learning songs. If you are a guitar player, it's even easier. You can use any MIDI track, whether it is a guitar track or not, and make a guitar tablature file. This is an easy way to learn difficult riffs. To create a guitar TAB from a MIDI file or MIDI track, use the following procedure:

1. Open the project you want to use to create the guitar tablature, or if you have a .mid file, import it into a new project.
2. Select the track you want to generate the tablature from.
3. Choose View > Staff from the SONAR menu. The Staff view appears with all of the track's data selected (see Figure 5.8).

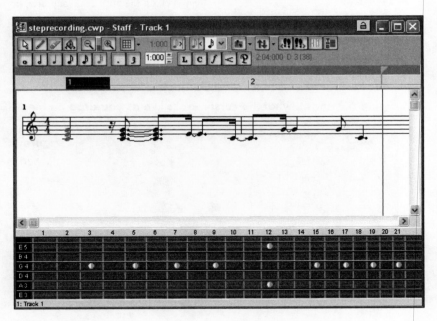

Figure 5.8

The Staff view.

4. If the Fretboard pane is not already open, click the Show/Hide Fretboard button in the Staff view. The Staff view now appears as it does in Figure 5.9, with the Fretboard pane at the bottom of the Staff view.

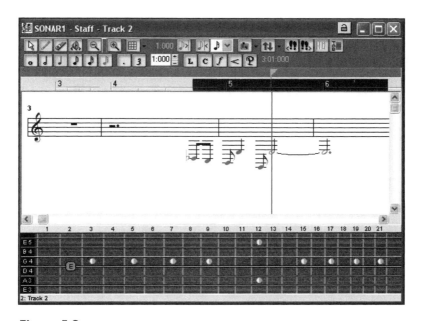

Figure 5.9

The Staff view with the Fretboard pane displayed.

5. Right-click in an empty space in the Staff pane (over the Fretboard pane) and choose Regenerate Tablature from the menu that appears (see Figure 5.10).

Figure 5.10

The Regenerate Tablature dialog box.

6. Adjust the settings in the Regenerate Tablature dialog box. For best results, use the Floating setting first and see how the tablature looks. If you are not satisfied, for example if the notes are all over the fretboard and the resulting tablature doesn't look possible to play, try the Fixed setting and confine the tablature to the number of frets comfortable for you. You may have to tweak these settings and regenerate the tablature several times before you get a result you are happy with.

7. Move the Now time to the beginning of the MIDI track in the Staff view and click the Play button.

8. Watch the Fretboard view to see if the notes are playable.

9. If it looks like the notes are playable, click the TAB button in the Staff view. The Save As dialog box appears.

10. Enter a name and navigate to where you want to save the file. Click Save.

Creating Drum Parts

The Piano Roll view's Pattern Brush tool is a flexible and simple solution to creating drum tracks quickly. SONAR comes with many patterns out of the box and you can create your own, either from scratch or existing .mid files. The following two tips show you how to use and create patterns using the Pattern Brush tool.

Adding Rolls and Fills to a Track

SONAR has a bunch of rolls and fills ready to be added to your MIDI tracks using the Pattern Brush tool. The Pattern Brush is designed with drums in mind, although it doesn't strictly have to be for that purpose. Patterns can be tied to note values (drum sounds) and note times, or simply note times, allowing you to pick which drums sounds you want to use. The following procedure shows you how to add a drum fill to a MIDI track:

1. Assign a MIDI track's output to a new or existing drum map.

2. Select the drum sounds you want to use. The SONAR 5 Help shows you how to do this if you do not know how.

3. Open the MIDI track in the Piano Roll view.

4. Click the arrow to the right of the Pattern Brush tool and select a fill pattern (see Figure 5.11).

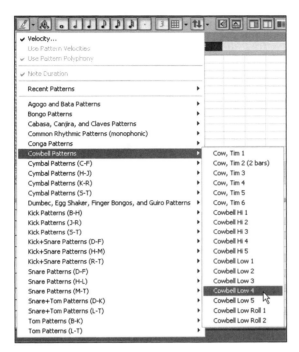

Figure 5.11

Selecting a fill pattern.

5. Click that same arrow again and choose if you want to use the pattern's velocities (Use Pattern Velocities).

6. Click that same arrow yet again and choose if you want to use the pattern's note information (Use Pattern Polyphony).

7. Click the Pattern Brush button to select it.

8. Drag the Pattern Brush over the section where you want to add the fill. See an example of a fill added to a MIDI track in Figure 5.12.

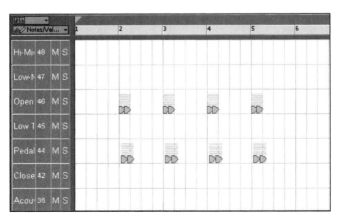

Figure 5.12

A drum pattern added to a track using the Pattern Brush.

Creating Custom Drum Patterns for the Pattern Brush

You are not limited to the Pattern Brush parts included with SONAR; you can create your own. To do so:

1. Create a file with a single MIDI track.
2. Create a marker in the Time Ruler where you want the pattern to start and name the marker what you want the pattern to be called.
3. At the end of the pattern, create a marker called "end." See Figure 5.13.

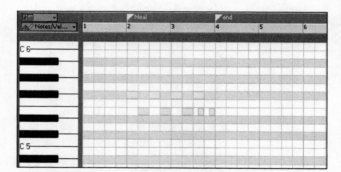

Figure 5.13

A single pattern defined by markers in a MIDI track.

4. Save the file as a .mid file in the directory where you store your patterns. The default directory is Pattern Brush Patterns in the root directory where you installed SONAR.

You can create multiple patterns in a single track by creating a new marker at the end of the previous pattern. Use the end marker after the last pattern. See Figure 5.14.

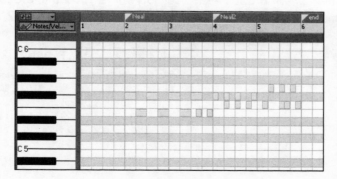

Figure 5.14

Multiple patterns defined by markers in a MIDI track.

Making All Your Edits in the Piano Roll View Without Switching Tools

The Piano Roll view is cleverly designed. It allows you to perform nearly every edit imaginable using a single tool. Using a number of modifier keys you can add, edit, move and edit the parameters of your notes. The following procedure tells you how:

1. Open a MIDI track in the Piano Roll view.
2. Select the Draw tool.
3. Enter or edit notes according to Table 5.2.

Table 5.2 Editing Notes in the Piano Roll View Using Only the Draw Tool

To Do This	Do This
Add a note	Click where you want a note.
Delete a note	Alt-click the note you want to delete.
Move a note in time	Move the cursor over a note until the cursor changes to look like it does in Figure 5.15 and drag the note to its new location.
Change a note's pitch	Move the cursor over a note until the cursor changes to look like it does in Figure 5.15 and drag the note up or down.
Change a note's start time	Move the cursor over the beginning of a note until the cursor changes to look like it does in Figure 5.16 and drag the beginning of the note to its new location. If you want to keep the note the same length, move the note instead of changing its start time. Moving the start time also increases or decreases the length of the note.
Change a note's end time	Move the cursor over the end of a note until the cursor changes to look like it does in Figure 5.16 and drag the end of the note to its new location.

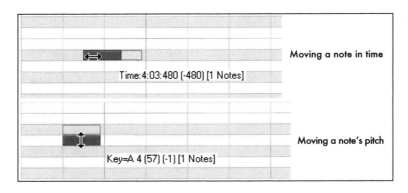

Moving a note in time

Time:4:03:480 (-480) [1 Notes]

Moving a note's pitch

Key=A 4 (57) [-1] [1 Notes]

Figure 5.15

Editing note time and pitch.

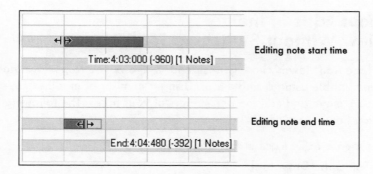

Figure 5.16

Editing a note's start and end time.

You can also use the Draw tool to edit controller data in the Controllers pane. Right-clicking on a note also brings up the Note Properties dialog box (see Figure 5.17).

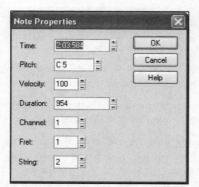

Figure 5.17

The Note Properties dialog box.

Snapping MIDI Notes to the Current Scale

SONAR 5 lets you assign a scale to a track and prohibits you from adding or moving a note to any of the notes not in that scale. No more notes accidentally placed in the wrong place. The following two tips cover using Snap to Scale and creating your own scales.

Using Snap to Scale

Enable the Snap to Scale feature using the following procedure:

1. In a MIDI track, click the Snap to Scale button (see Figure 5.18).
2. Select a Scale from the Scale menu.
3. Select a Root note from the Root note menu. This is the key of your scale.

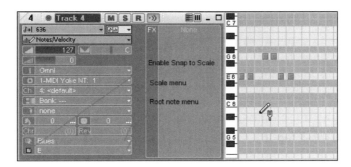

Figure 5.18
The Snap to Scale button, Scale menu, and Root note menu in a MIDI track.

4. Enter notes in the track. Notice a tuning fork appears next to your cursor and non-scale notes are grayed out.

Creating a Custom Scale

SONAR 5 has more scales than you knew existed, but if you feel the need to create something unique, you can create your own scale. To do so:

1. Click on the Scale menu (see Figure 5.18) and choose Scale Manager from the menu.
2. In the Scale Manager, in the Scale Family field, choose Custom User Scales.
3. In the Scales field, enter a name for your scale and click the New button to the right.
4. Click on the notes on the keyboard to the left or on the buttons at the bottom to select the notes you want for your scale (see Figure 5.19).
5. Click OK.

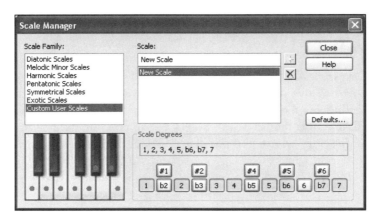

Figure 5.19
The Scale Manager dialog box.

Quick Chord Transposition Using Snap to Scale

If you decide to change keys and want to transpose all of your chords to the new key, the Snap to Scale feature can help you move all your notes while retaining the original chord structure (that is, your major chords will still be major chords). To do so:

1. Select the track whose chords you want to transpose.
2. Enable the Snap to Scale feature (see "Using the Snap to Scale" to see how).
3. Select a scale in the Scale menu.
4. Select the new key in the Root Note menu.
5. Select the track to select all the MIDI chords in the track.
6. Hold down the Shift key to preserve the note's timing and drag the data so the old root note is on the new root note. Release. See Figure 5.20.

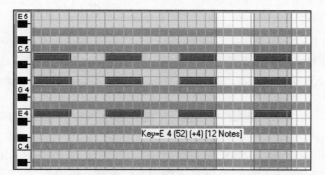

Figure 5.20
Dragging all chords in a track to a new key.

The notes in the chords snap to the available notes in the scale, preserving the chords' structure.

Editing MIDI with CAL

CAL (Cakewalk Application Language) is not really discussed much, other than by those who have used Cakewalk for many years. There are some pretty handy scripts out there. The following two tips show you how to use a few very handy CAL scripts that ship with SONAR. You can find them in the Sample Content directory where you installed SONAR 5.

Splitting MIDI Drums into Multiple Tracks

The CAL script Split notes to Tracks.CAL splits MIDI drums into a track for each instrument. To use this script:

1. Open a MIDI drum track that has multiple instruments on it.
2. Choose Process > Run CAL from the SONAR menu. The Open dialog box appears. The Open dialog box should automatically open to where your CAL scripts have been installed.
3. Select Split Notes to Tracks.CAL.
4. Select a script and click OK.
5. A series of dialog boxes asks for the following:
   ❋ Source Track—Enter the number of the track you want to split into multiple tracks (see Figure 5.21).

Figure 5.21
The Source Track dialog box.

   ❋ First Destination Track—Enter the number of the track where you want the first new track to appear (see Figure 5.22).

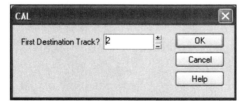

Figure 5.22
The First Destination Track dialog box.

   ❋ Destination Channel—Enter the channel number you want to use for the new track's tracks (see Figure 5.23).

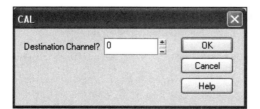

Figure 5.23
The Destination Channel dialog box.

❋ Destination Port—Enter the port number you want to use for the new track's tracks (see Figure 5.24).

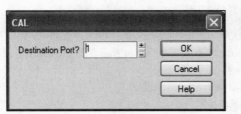

Figure 5.24
The Destination Port dialog box.

The new tracks appear in order, beginning with the track number you entered for the First Destination Track. See Figure 5.25.

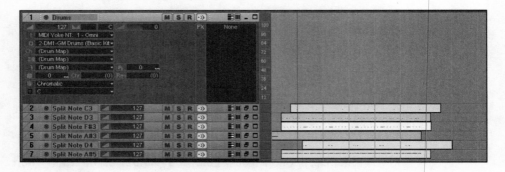

Figure 5.25
Tracks created after the Split Notes to Tracks.CAL script was run.

Randomize Velocity to Humanize a MIDI Track

Editing the velocity of each note to make it feel more natural isn't an option if you want to finish a project in your lifetime, but a CAL script called VaryVel.CAL can do it for you in a few seconds. To use the script:

1. Select the track on which you want to randomize the velocities.
2. If you want just a selection of notes to be affected by the script, select a range in the Time Ruler.
3. Choose Process > Run CAL.
4. Select the VaryVel.CAL script and click Open.
5. Two dialog boxes ask you for a range of acceptable velocities:
   ❋ Low Limit of Velocity Range—Enter the lowest velocity you want on the selected track (see Figure 5.26).

Figure 5.26
The Low Limit of Velocity Range dialog box.

❋ High Limit of Velocity Range—Enter the highest velocity you want on the selected track (see Figure 5.27).

Figure 5.27
The High Limit of Velocity Range dialog box.

A message box appears, giving you the results of the velocity changes (see Figure 5.28).

6. Click OK.

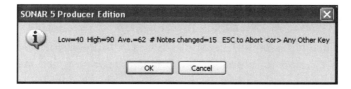

Figure 5.28
Message box showing the results of the VaryVel.CAL script on a track.

Create Chords from a Single MIDI Note

There are a series of CAL scripts that can transform a note or a number of notes into the root of a chord. You can quickly transform a simple melody into a rich arrangement of chords. To do so:

1. Select a note or series of notes in a MIDI track. You can select contiguous notes by selecting a time range in the Time Ruler, or you can select a note and select additional notes while holding down the Ctrl key.

2. Choose Process > Run CAL from the SONAR menu.

3. Select one of the following scripts in the Open dialog box:

❋ Dominant 7th Chord.CAL

❋ Major 7th Chord.CAL

❋ Major Chord.CAL

❋ Minor 7th Chord.CAL

❋ Minor Chord.CAL

4. Click Open.

The Script runs, creating the chord's additional notes above the root (see Figure 5.29).

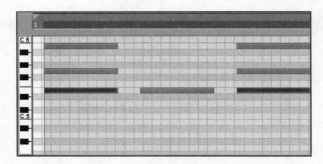

Figure 5.29

Two selected notes after being processed with Major Chord.CAL.

Modify Scripts to Expand Chord Options

The basic chord types provided out of the box in SONAR are just the beginning. The CAL scripts for creating chords from a root note are very basic and you can copy and modify them to create other chord types. To do so:

1. Copy one of the scripts listed in the preceding tip and give it a new name based on what chord you want to create. Our example is Diminished Chord.CAL and we begin by using the Minor 7th Chord.CAL script.

2. Open the script in Notepad, or any text editor. Figure 5.30 shows the script as it looks in Notepad.

3. Change the Note.Key values in the second and third lines from 7 and 10 to 6 and 9, as seen in Figure 5.31.

4. Save the file.

There are many other CAL scripts you can modify for your own needs, but they may already exist. There are several sites on the Internet that have a library of free scripts you can download and primers on learning CAL programming. A quick search for "Cakewalk Application Language" can get you started.

```
(do
        (include "need20.cal") ; Require version 2.0 or higher of CAL

        (forEachEvent
            (if (== Event.Kind NOTE)
                (do
                    (insert Event.Time Event.Chan NOTE (+ Note.Key  3) Note.Vel Note.Dur)
                    (insert Event.Time Event.Chan NOTE (+ Note.Key  7) Note.Vel Note.Dur)
                    (insert Event.Time Event.Chan NOTE (+ Note.Key 10) Note.Vel Note.Dur)
                )
            )
        )
)
```

Figure 5.30

The Minor 7th Chord.CAL script.

```
(do
        (include "need20.cal")  ; Require version 2.0 or higher of CAL

        (forEachEvent
            (if (== Event.Kind NOTE)
                (do
                    (insert Event.Time Event.Chan NOTE (+ Note.Key  3) Note.Vel Note.Dur)
                    (insert Event.Time Event.Chan NOTE (+ Note.Key  6) Note.Vel Note.Dur)
                    (insert Event.Time Event.Chan NOTE (+ Note.Key  9) Note.Vel Note.Dur)
                )
            )
        )
)
```

Figure 5.31

New script called Diminished Chord.CAL.

Vertically Maximizing a MIDI Track in the Track View Instantly

Fitting all of a track's MIDI notes into the available space is easy with
SONAR's Fit Content command. To use the Fit Content command:

1. Right-click the splitter bar between the Track pane and the Clips pane.
   Figure 5.32 shows the MIDI track before you use the Fit Content
   command.

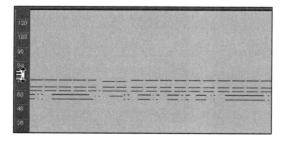

Figure 5.32

A tracks MIDI data before
using the Fit Content command.

2. Choose Fit Content from the menu that appears. Figure 5.33 shows the result of the Fit Content command.

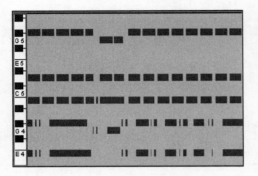

Figure 5.33

A track's MIDI data after using the Fit Content command.

Modifying an Unlimited Number of Notes in Seconds

If, after carefully recording or entering hundreds or thousands of MIDI notes in a project, you suddenly want to change all of the dozens of A naturals to A sharps, the task might seem daunting. It need not be, because SONAR has the capability to search and replace MIDI data according to the criteria you enter. To do so:

1. Select the track or a part of the track on which you want to search and replace data.

2. Choose Process > Interpolate from the SONAR menu. The Event Filter—Search dialog box appears.

3. Deselect all but the Notes check box.

4. In the Notes Min and Max fields, enter the note you want to change followed by the octave range. If for example, the A natural notes appear between the third and sixth octaves, you enter A 3 in the Minimum field and A 6 in the Maximum field. See Figure 5.34.

5. Click OK. The Event Filter—Replace dialog box appears.

6. In the Notes Min and Max fields, enter A#3 and A#6 respectively. See Figure 5.35.

7. Click OK.

8. Examine the project closely to make sure the results are what you expected before saving the file.

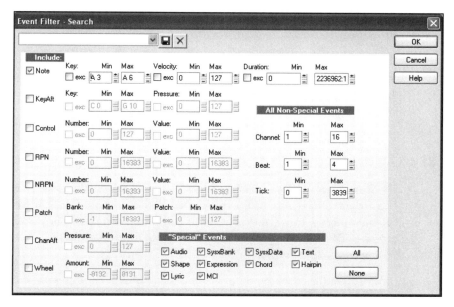

Figure 5.34

The Event Filter—Search dialog box.

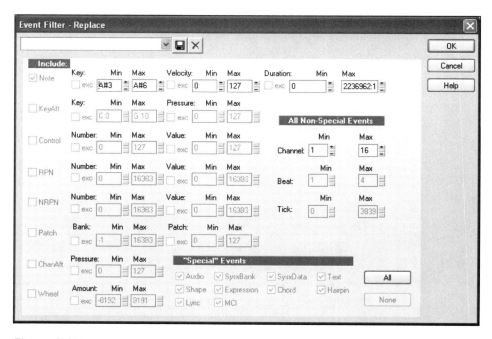

Figure 5.35

The Event Filter—Replace dialog box.

SONAR searches the selection for the A natural notes and replaces them with A# notes.

The Interpolate command is very powerful. You can search for and replace nearly any MIDI parameter, including RPNs and NRPNs. A little time reading the Help for Interpolate and playing with this feature can lead to a lot of your time being saved.

Quickly Cleaning Up Your MIDI Recordings

The beauty of MIDI recording is that it is a lot easier to clean up than audio. The Deglitch filter makes it even easier. You can search your MIDI recording for quiet notes, short notes, or notes out of the range of the part you are playing. Deglitch is very handy for eliminating accidentally played notes. To use the Deglitch filter:

1. Select the track or a part of the track on which you want to search and replace data.

2. Choose Process > Deglitch from the SONAR menu. The Deglitch dialog box appears (see Figure 5.36).

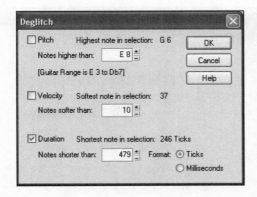

Figure 5.36

The Deglitch dialog box with a minimum duration set to just under an eighth note.

3. Do one or more of the following:
   - ❋ Check the Pitch check box and set a maximum allowed pitch in the Notes Higher Than field.
   - ❋ Check the Velocity check box and set a minimum allowed velocity in the Notes Softer Than field.
   - ❋ Check the Duration check box and set a minimum allowed duration in the Notes Shorter Than field.

4. Click OK.

5. Check your track or selection to make sure no MIDI notes you wanted to keep have been deleted.

Modifying the Piano Roll View Using .INI Variables

There are a series of .ini variables you can add to cakewalk.ini. The following five tips involve using variables to adjust the appearance of notes and controller data in the Piano Roll view.

Show Velocity as a Bar Graph

Velocity data in the Controller pane of the Piano Roll view appears as a solid line (see Figure 5.37).

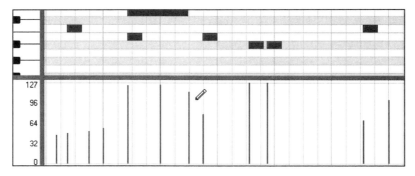

Figure 5.37

Default appearance of velocity data in the Controller pane of the Piano Roll view.

You can use an .ini variable to change it to a bar graph. To do so:

1. Exit SONAR if it is running.

2. Navigate to where you installed SONAR 5.

3. In the SONAR 5 folder, open the Cakewalk.ini file using Notepad or any text editor.

4. Add the following line to the section [WinCake]:

   VelocityAsBargraph=1

   See Figure 5.38 for how it looks in the Cakewalk.ini file.

5. Save cakewalk.ini.

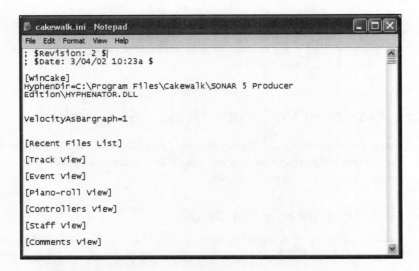

Figure 5.38

The `VelocityAsBargraph` line added to Cakewalk.ini.

If you want to revert to the default appearance, change the 1 to a 0 (zero), or delete the line completely.

Open SONAR and see the difference (see Figure 5.39).

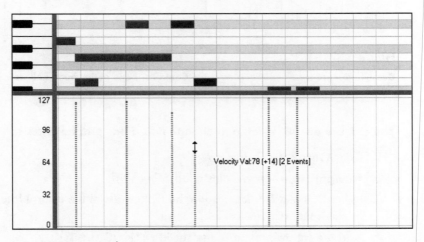

Figure 5.39

Appearance of velocity data with the `VelocityAsBargraph` variable enabled.

You can add another variable to the cakewalk.ini file to make the width of the velocity bars the same as the note lengths. Go to the next tip if you want to change the width of the velocity bar graph.

Make the Width of the Velocity Bar Graph the Note Length

If you have added the `VelocityAsBargraph` variable to the cakewalk.ini file, you can add another variable to the cakewalk.ini file to change the width of the velocity data. Using this variable, the appearance of the velocity data is similar to Cakewalk's Project5, version 1 (see Figure 5.40). To increase the width of the bar graph notes, use the procedure from the previous tip to add the following variable to cakewalk.ini (see Figure 5.41):

```
VelocityBargraphFullWidth=1
```

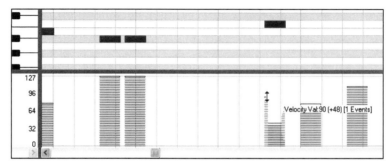

Figure 5.40

The appearance of velocity data with the `VelocityBargraphFullWidth` variable enabled.

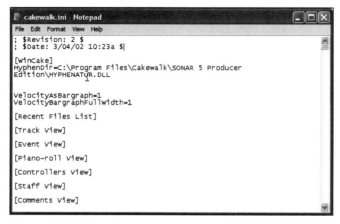

Figure 5.41

The `VelocityBargraphFullWidth` line in the Cakewalk.ini file.

If you want to disable this variable, change the 1 to a 0 (zero), or delete the line completely. If the full note width is too wide for you, you can increase the width of the velocity data by a few pixels. The next tip shows you how.

Set the Pixel Width for the Velocity Bar Graph

If you have not changed the appearance of your velocity data, you can double its width. To do so, follow the procedure from the previous tip, "Show Velocity as a Bar Graph," to add the following line to cakewalk.ini (see Figure 5.42):

```
VelocitySolidWidth=4
```

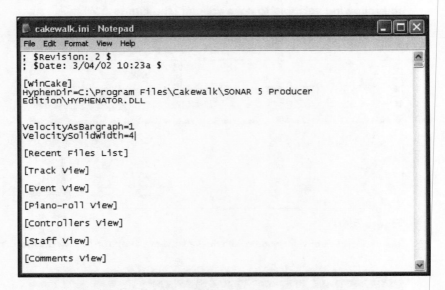

Figure 5.42

The VelocitySolidWidth line in the Cakewalk.ini file.

The number represents the number of pixels. The possible values are 2 (the default), 3, and 4. If you want to disable this variable, change the 1 to a 0 (zero), or delete the line completely. To see how this variable looks, see Figure 5.43.

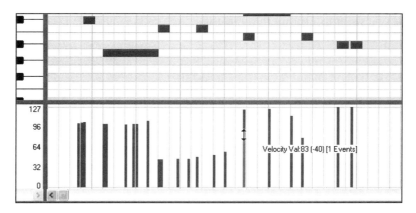

Figure 5.43
Velocity data set to a width of four pixels.

Reduce the Size of the Velocity Line When the Note Height Is Reduced

If you have not changed the appearance of your velocity data, you can set the velocity data to appear thinner when the Piano Roll view has been zoomed out, thus making the note heights shorter. To do so, follow the procedure from the previous tip "Show Velocity as a Bar Graph," and add the following line to cakewalk.ini (see Figure 5.44):

```
VelocityAutoshrinkWidth=0
```

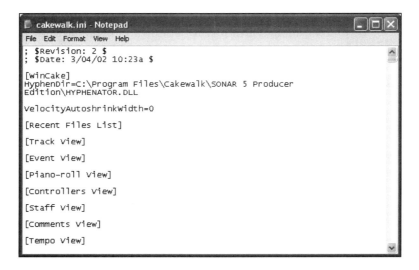

Figure 5.44
The VelocityAutoShrinkWidth line in the Cakewalk.ini.

If you want to disable this variable, change the 1 to a 0 (zero), or delete the line completely.

Use the Track Foreground Color for Notes in the Piano Roll View

If you want your MIDI notes to appear using the default foreground color rather than the background color, you can do so in the cakewalk.ini file. To do so, follow the procedure from the tip "Show Velocity as a Bar Graph," and add the following line to cakewalk.ini (see Figure 5.45):

```
PRVUseForegroundColor=0
```

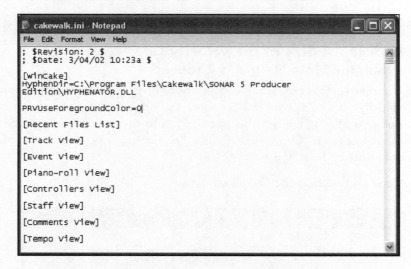

Figure 5.45

The PRVUseForegroundColor line in the Cakewalk.ini file.

If you want to disable this variable, change the 1 to a 0 (zero), or delete the line completely.

6 Virtual Instruments and Effects

Effects and virtual instruments (DXis and VSTs) offer you the capability to expand SONAR to handle nearly any signal processing task. From creating new sounds with samplers and synthesizers to reshaping your recordings with elaborate effects processors, these effects and instruments are more than just accessories.

This chapter shows you some of the ways you can get the most out of both your audio effects and your VSTs and DXis.

Bypassing Multiple Effects Bins at the Same Time

Opening each track one at a time to bypass your effects bins is time consuming, and unnecessary. You can bypass as many effects bins as you want with one command. To do so:

1. Select the tracks whose effects bins you want to bypass.
2. Right-click on one of the tracks selected.
3. Choose Bypass Effects Bin from the menu that appears (see Figure 6.1).

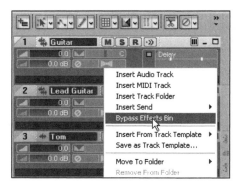

Figure 6.1
The Bypass Effects Bin command.

When bypassed, effects bins appear in a lighter shade of gray (see Figure 6.2) when using the default color scheme.

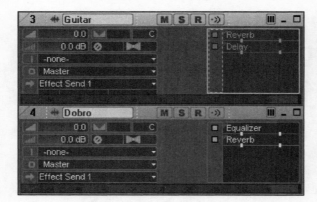

Figure 6.2

A bypassed bin—in the top track—and a track with an active effects bin.

Compensating for External Processor Latency

If you are sending a signal out of your audio interface, through an external processor, and then back into your sound card, it's likely the returning signal is out of sync with the rest of your audio. This added latency has to be fixed. A little simple math is all it takes to adjust your audio tracks that have been run through an external processor. Use the following procedure for each external processor. You can use the value you get for each to adjust the timing of the track accordingly.

1. Make sure the original track you are going to process is on a measure or sizeable beat boundary (quarter, 8th, 16th, or 32nd).
2. Set the output of a track to the one connected to your external processor.
3. Set the output of your external processor to one of your audio card inputs. Careful, don't create a feedback loop!
4. Record the processed audio to a new track. See Figure 6.3 for how that might appear in the Track view.
5. Zoom in all the way on the beginning of the original clip.
6. Right-click on the Time Ruler and choose Time Ruler Format > Samples.
7. Write down the sample number when the original clip begins.
8. Repeat these steps for the track you ran through the external processor.
9. Subtract the second track from the first.

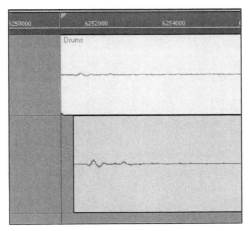

Figure 6.3

Latency between original and externally processed track.

10. Right-click on the original track.
11. Choose Clip Properties from the menu that appears.
12. In the Clip Properties dialog box, enter the value from step 8 in the Snap Offset field (see Figure 6.4).

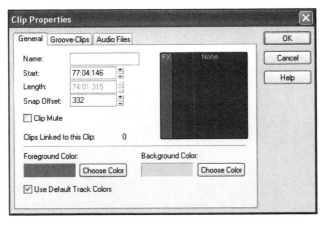

Figure 6.4

Entering the Snap Offset value in the processed clip.

13. In the Snap To Grid dialog box, set the Snap to Musical time and choose the coarsest setting possible; that is, if the beginning clip starts on a whole measure, use whole, if it begins on the 3rd beat, use half, and so on (see Figure 6.5). Make sure the Move To option is selected.
14. With Snap enabled, drag your clip and release it when the Snap Offset line is about where the original clip begins. The clip should snap right in place (as it does in Figure 6.6).

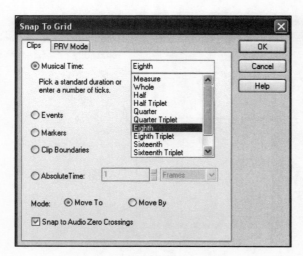

Figure 6.5

The Snap to Grid dialog box.

Now your processed clip is lined up with the beginning of the original clip.

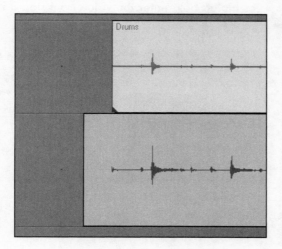

Figure 6.6

Clips lined up.

Frequency Modulation Using Delay

Frequency modulation is a form of processing that can create and amplify sidebands in audio. By using a delay effect with a very small repeat time and a moderate to high feedback as a modulator, you can achieve anything from a gritty lo-fi sound to a bell-like chime.

1. Start with an audio source that contains a wide range of frequencies and harmonics. Percussion works quite well.

2. Insert an EQ into the signal chain—any EQ with suitable shelving or peak filters will do.

3. Insert a Delay such as the Sonitus Delay or FxDelay. Set initial parameters as follows:

   ❊ Set Mix level to 100% so you are monitoring only the delayed signal.

   ❊ Raise the feedback to about 90% or so.

   ❊ Lower the delay time to 0.0 ms. If the delay is set to match host tempo, switch it to a manual mode that gives you precise control.

   ❊ Turn off any stereo cross-feed controls.

4. Raise the delay amount as slowly as possible until you hear a change in the tone.

5. Raise the feedback to 97% to 99% (see Figure 6.7). On some delay effects, you can raise it to 100% safely, whereas on others it may lead to constant feedback.

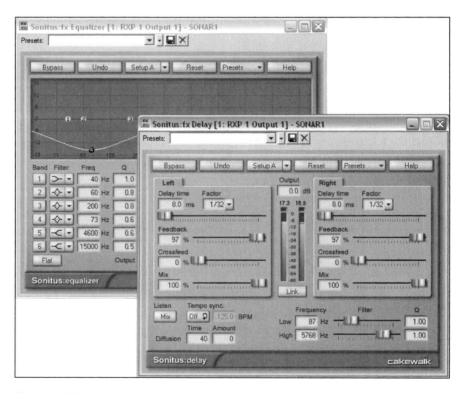

Figure 6.7

Feedback raised to 97%.

6. Right-click on the audio track and choose Envelopes > Create Track Envelope and select the delay time or fine-tune options on your delay.

7. Create several nodes and snap them to beats or measures. Right-click the envelope between nodes and choose jump (see Figure 6.8).

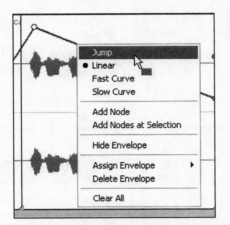

Figure 6.8
The Jump command.

8. Adjust the envelope between the nodes to change sideband frequencies.

9. Now use the EQ you patched in to emphasize certain frequencies or to roll off extreme highs or lows in order to bring out more harmonics.

Adding Depth to Drum Parts Using Delay

Part of creating interesting drum parts, whether you are programming them or playing them, involves creating complexity and rhythmic nuance. One way to achieve this is through the use of *ghost notes*—which are very quiet notes used to emphasize the preceding or following note. When working with loops or dry-sound drums, this technique can add more excitement.

Rather than reprogramming the drums or creating a different loop, you can use the existing pattern by using delay. By adjusting the mix level, you affect the volume of the ghost notes and by adjusting delay time, you affect the *swing* imposed by the ghost notes.

1. Insert a delay on the drum track. It doesn't matter if it follows the host tempo or not; in fact, it is preferred that it has a manual mode.

2. Use a delay calculator (such as the one from AnalogX http://www.analogx.com/contents/download/audio/delay.htm) to calculate the amount of time that corresponds to a quarter note at your current tempo, if the plug-in you are using does not have one built in.

3. Set the mix level to 10% and feedback to 0%. Play the drum track and adjust the mix level to between 10% and 30%. Keep the feedback at under 10%.

4. Adjust the coarse timing by quarter notes and adjust the timing by milliseconds to achieve a subtle swing in the sound.

Instead of using the effect as an insert, patch it to a bus and run an aux send from the track to that bus. Now set the mix level to 100% wet and route the original track and bus into a new bus. Routing the effect this way gives you new possibilities:

❈ EQ: Try placing an EQ on the original track before the delay and on the bus to emphasize or roll off certain frequencies. For example, removing some of the bass frequencies from the delay signal will make the results less muddy and prevent them from interfering with the kick drum's groove. Rolling off some of the high-end to emphasize the mids can emulate the sound of a tape delay.

Some Delay plug-ins, such as the Sonitus delay, may already have EQ or filtering built in (see Figure 6.9).

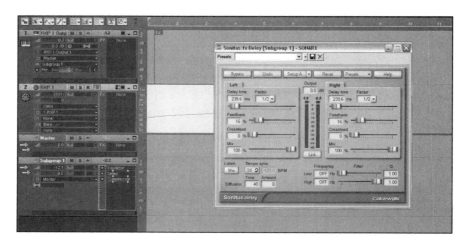

Figure 6.9

Low and High frequency filters in Sonitus:fx Delay.

❅ Compression: Compressing the delayed signal can emphasize different hits than in the original. You can even set a compressor on the original as well with different settings. You may want to try using heavy compression on the delayed signal to equalize the levels by using a low threshold, a ratio of 8:1 or higher, and then setting the makeup gain accordingly.

When using timings that correspond very closely with the exact quarter, eighth note, and higher mix settings, take care to ensure that you are not getting phasing with any of the hits.

Mastering V-Vocal

As of version 5, SONAR has a vocal processing utility called V-Vocal, which is based on Roland's Vary-Phrase technology. It has the power to correct pitch, adjust the timing of phrases, and even create harmony vocal parts. V-Vocal is applied to a clip, creating V-Vocal clips, which you can edit using various tools, or enable automatic pitch correction.

Correcting Pitch Using V-Vocal

V-Vocal does a good job in "automatic" mode, but let's look at fixing a single phrase using the V-Vocal tools. There are a few tricks to getting the most natural sounding pitch correction.

To correct the pitch using V-Vocal:

1. In the Track view, right-click on the clip on which you want to correct the pitch.
2. Choose V-Vocal > Create V-Vocal Clip from the menu that appears. V-Vocal appears.
3. Select the Arrow tool (see Figure 6.10).
4. Use the Arrow tool to adjust individual pitches (see Figure 6.11).
5. Select the Vibrato/LFO tool (see Figure 6.12).
6. Use the Vibrato/LFO tool to decrease the variation of the note's pitch (see Figure 6.13).
7. Select the Curve tool (see Figure 6.14).
8. Use the Curve tool to remove oddities and smooth transitions from one note to another (see Figure 6.15).

Figure 6.10

The V-Vocal Arrow tool.

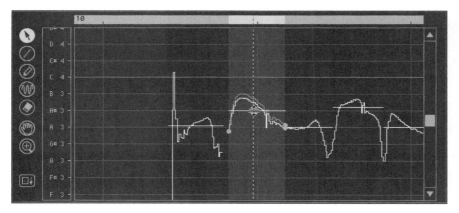

Figure 6.11

Adjusting the pitch of a note in V-Vocal using the Arrow tool.

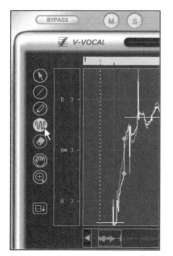

Figure 6.12

The Vibrato/LFO tool.

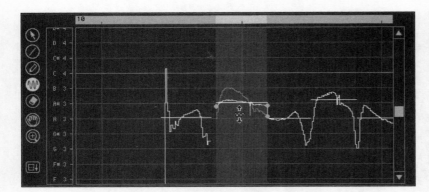

Figure 6.13
Leveling the pitch variation in V-Vocal using the Waveform tool.

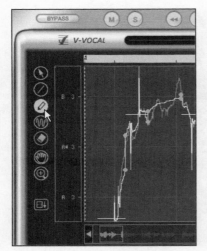

Figure 6.14
The Curve tool.

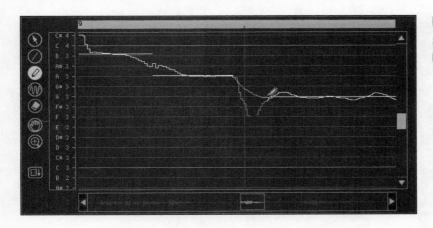

Figure 6.15
Smoothing the transition between notes in V-Vocal.

Fixing Timing Issues Using V-Vocal

V-Vocal is an excellent tool for fixing timing in a part, and not just a vocal part. You can make timing adjustments to nearly any track. To do so:

1. In the Track view, right-click on the clip on which you want to correct the timing.
2. Choose V-Vocal > Create V-Vocal Clip from the menu that appears. V-Vocal appears.
3. Click the Time button at the bottom of V-Vocal (see Figure 6.16).

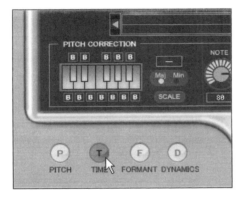

Figure 6.16
The Time button.

4. Select the Arrow tool and click where you want to move the waveform (see Figure 6.17).
5. Drag to where you want to begin or end the audio (see Figure 6.18).

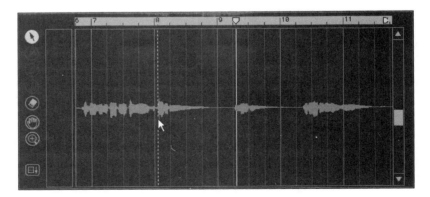

Figure 6.17
Waveform in V-Vocal before timing is edited.

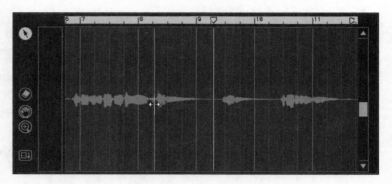

Figure 6.18

Waveform in V-Vocal with edited timing.

Writing Harmony Parts with V–Vocal

For those of you like me, who can't harmonize by ear, V-Vocal can help you write harmony parts. With a little tweaking, these parts are usable. Re-recording a vocal based on a harmony generated by V-Vocal can humanize the part. The following procedure is for creating a single vocal harmony line:

1. Select the vocal track you want to create a harmony vocal for.

2. Choose Track > Clone from the SONAR menu.

3. In the cloned track, right-click the clip to which you want to add a harmony part.

4. Choose V-Vocal > Create V-Vocal Clip from the menu that appears. V-Vocal appears.

5. Using the Arrow tool, drag each note up by a major third (see Figure 6.19).

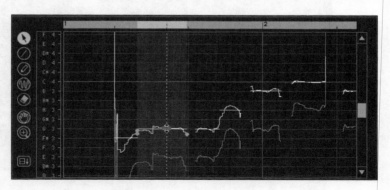

Figure 6.19

Using the Arrow tool to raise the pitch of a note by a major third.

6. Loop the V-Vocal clip.

7. While the loop is playing, adjust the Shift knob in the Formants section until you find the most natural sounding setting (see Figure 6.20).

Figure 6.20

The Shift knob.

8. Adjust the Pitch Follow knob in the Formants section until you find the most natural setting.

9. Repeat steps 7 and 8 until you are satisfied with the results.

10. Either keep the V-Vocal parts or sing the parts yourself.

Adding Vibrato Using V-Vocal

Whether or not you use V-Vocal to correct pitch or timing in a clip, you may want to use it for adding vibrato to a note or two. A subtle warble in a voice, especially in a long help note, can add a lot of depth and feeling to a vocal. To add vibrato using V-Vocal:

1. In the Track view, right-click on the clip on which you want to add vibrato.

2. Choose V-Vocal > Create V-Vocal Clip from the menu that appears. V-Vocal appears.

3. Select the Vibrato/LFO tool and hold it over the beginning of where you want to add vibrato in the clip.

4. The cursor changes to look like it does in Figure 6.21.

5. Click and drag over the portion of clip you want to affect. If you hold down the Ctrl key while dragging, you limit the vibrato to just amplitude. If you hold down the Shift key while dragging, you limit the vibrato to just frequency.

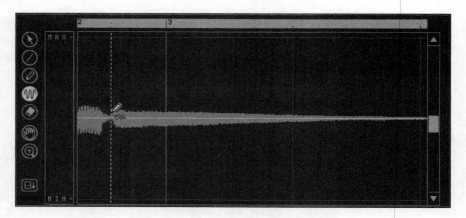

Figure 6.21

The cursor as it looks when you are ready to draw vibrato.

6. You can edit the depth of the vibrato using the Waveform tool. You can also fade in the vibrato by holding the cursor at the beginning of the vibrato section until the cursor changes to look like it does in Figure 6.22 and dragging it over the vibrato section. Move the cursor up or down to increase or decrease the vibrato's depth at the end of the section.

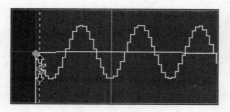

Figure 6.22

The cursor as it looks when you are ready to edit vibrato depth.

Using Sonitus:fx Equalizer to Create a Cheap Radio Effect

An interesting effect for the first verse of a song is to make it sound small, like it's coming through a bad radio, and then kick in the song in all its glory. The difference makes the song sound that much fuller. Also, you can hear this effect used on vocals to good effect, often panned and delayed as an echo. It is an easy effect to create.

1. Right-click in your track or bus effects bin and choose Sonitus:fx > Equalizer from the menu that appears.
2. In the Sonitus:fx Equalizer, set the Q for band 1 to about .7.

3. Drag the yellow dot for band 1 all the way down to –18dB and to the 250Hz mark.
4. Set the Q for band 6 to about .7.
5. Drag the yellow dot for band 6 all the way down to –18dB and to the 4KHz mark.

When you are done, it should like something like Figure 6.23.

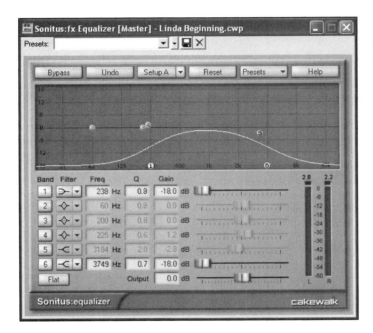

Figure 6.23

Sonitus:fx Equalizer settings for a "cheap radio" effect.

Copying Effects to Other Tracks or Busses

If you have an effect that you are happy with and want to do the same things with other tracks, you don't have to re-patch the effect in other tracks, open it and adjust settings, or apply a preset. You can use the Ctrl key as a modifier to drag a copy to another effects bin. To copy an effect to another track or bus:

1. Hold down the Ctrl key and click on the effect you want to copy.
2. While holding the Ctrl key, drag the effect to the effects bin where you want it to be copied.

Creating a Reverse Reverb Effect

A reverse reverb lead-in on a vocal is a pretty cool effect (if used in moderation!), and it is pretty easily done in SONAR 5.

To create a reverse reverb lead-in for a vocal track:

1. Create a copy of the vocal track to which you want to add a reverse reverb lead-in.
2. In the copy of the vocal track, use the Split tool to create a clip of just the first phrase or line
3. Select the first phrase of the vocal part.
4. Choose Process > Audio > Reverse from the SONAR menu.
5. Right-click the reversed clip and choose Process Effect > Audio > Sonitus:fx > Reverb from the menu that appears.
6. In Sonitus:fx Reverb, create a reverb with a long, slow decay. Use the Audition button to listen to the effect.
7. Click OK to apply the effect.
8. Select the clip and use the Reverse command again.
9. Use the Split tool to cut the clip at the point when the original vocal begins.
10. Delete the latter part of the clip. Figure 6.24 shows how an original vocal clip and a clip with reverse reverb might look.
11. Play back your song and adjust volume and pan to your liking.

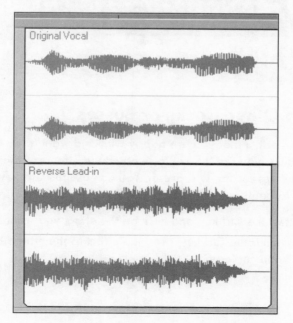

Figure 6.24

Original vocal track and the reverse reverb vocal below it.

Try keeping the reverse reverb track at a low volume and panned to one side for a nice subtle effect, or preserve the original pan and volume for a more in-your-face type of effect.

Replacing Drum Hits Using Cyclone

If you are into using drum loops but have trouble finding enough variety, you can turn any good loop into a few good loops using Cyclone DXi. Cyclone DXi lets you move slices of a loop around, creating a new loop. Follow this procedure to replace drum hits using Cyclone DXi.

1. Insert Cyclone in the Synth Rack.
2. Load a drum loop (Groove clip or ACIDized wave file).
3. Drag the loop name from the Loop bin to one of the pads.
4. Select the pad. The editable slices appear in the Pad Editor at the bottom of Cyclone. Selected slices display the corresponding section of the waveform in the Loop view (see Figure 6.25).

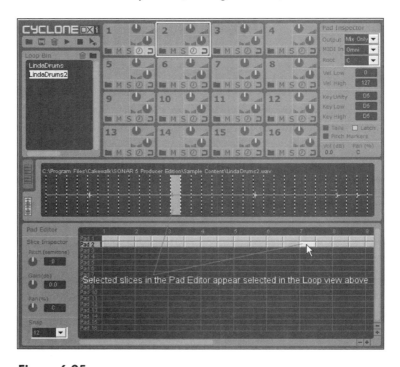

Figure 6.25

Highlighting a slice in the Pad Editor also highlights the portion of the loop in the Loop view.

5. Click and drag a slice to a new location in the sequence. In this case, you are dragging a harder snare hit over the existing lighter hit. If you shorten the loop, the loop continues until it hits the Track Handle. Move the track handle to the end of the last beat you want to hear (see Figure 6.26).

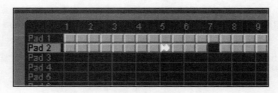

Figure 6.26

New drum loop created ending after the fourth beat.

6. Continue to experiment with Cyclone. For example, try the following:

   ❈ Move a drum hit to a separate pad and rout it to a different output for a unique sound.

   ❈ Alternate transposing beats up and down for a freaky effect.

   ❈ Split a short section of a track, enable looping, and tweak the loop in Cyclone.

Automating Effects Using MIDI

Even without a control surface, you can easily edit and record parameter changes for VST or DX effects. To do this, use the assignable widgets in the Track Inspector or Console view.

1. Right-click a slider and choose Reassign Control and then the property you want it to edit (see Figure 6.27).

2. Right-click again and choose Remote Control.

3. Move the knob, slider, or wheel you want to use and then click the Learn button in the Remote Control dialog box (see Figure 6.28).

To record automation, right-click on the control and choose Arm Parameter and use the Record Automation button in the transport.

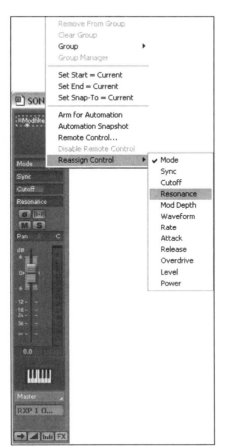

Figure 6.27

Options in the Reassign Control context menu.

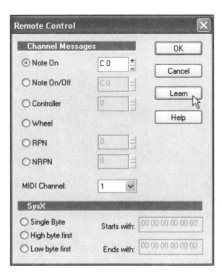

Figure 6.28

Remote Control dialog box.

Creating a Drum Machine from the MIDI Keyboard and Cyclone

You can create loops as short as a single beat in Cyclone DXi. You can also trigger those loops using a MIDI controller. All you need to do is round up a few excellent drum loops and you can create your own original parts. To do so:

1. Load up to 16 loops into the Loop bin and assign each to one of the 16 pads.

2. Select a pad.

3. In the Pad Editor (see Figure 6.29), drag the slice you want to use for the pad—a snare hit, for example, or a kick drum. If you want to have a pad trigger a short piece like a fill, drag the fill in order to the beginning of the loop.

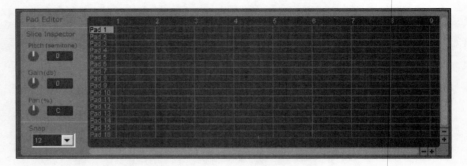

Figure 6.29
The Pad Editor in Cyclone DXi.

4. Move the Track Handle after the hit or fill (see Figure 6.30).

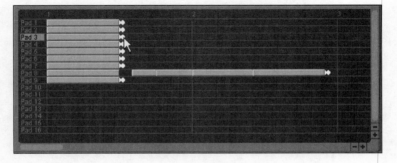

Figure 6.30
Nine pads each with a single hit or a short fill.

5. In the Pad Inspector, set the MIDI note or notes and note velocities that trigger the pad.

6. Repeat steps 2-5 for each pad.

You can now play your drum machine by playing SONAR and using your MIDI controller to trigger pads. If you want a note to loop over and over, set that pad to Latch mode. You might also need to experiment with the Track Handles to determine the best length of the loops.

Inserting an Effect on Individual Clips

If you are looking for an effect on a short piece of your audio, clip-based effects are the answer, especially if the effects you want to use are not automatable. Use the following procedure to apply an effect to just a small piece of a track.

1. Locate the part of a track you want to apply an effect on.

2. Using the Split tool, split the clip around where you want to apply the effect.

3. Right-click on the clip and choose Insert Effect > Audio > *effect name* or Insert Effect > MIDI > *effect name*.

An effects bin with the effect you inserted appears on the clip (see Figure 6.31).

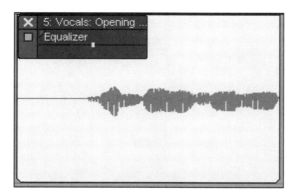

Figure 6.31
Clip with effect inserted.

Conserving CPU Cycles when Using Clip-Based Effects

Clip-based effects are handy, but using a lot of them can tax your CPU. If you find yourself using the same effect on multiple clips on the same track, there is a way to reduce the number of effect instances and thus use less of your computer's processing power. To do so:

1. Select all the clips in a track that use the same effect and effect settings. Split clips into smaller clips using the Split tool if necessary. You can Ctrl+click noncontiguous clips (see Figure 6.32).

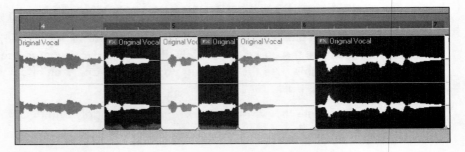

Figure 6.32

Clips selected.

2. Clone the original track and its settings, but not the events.
3. While holding down the Shift key, drag the selected clips onto the cloned track (see Figure 6.33).

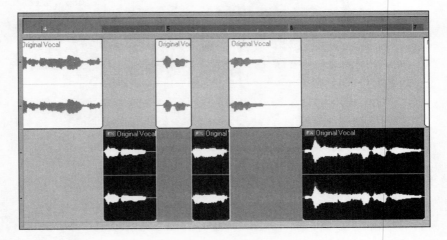

Figure 6.33

Dragging clips to the cloned track.

4. Ctrl+drag the effect from one of the clips to the FX bin of the cloned track.

5. Delete the effects instances from the clips.

Storing Effects Chains as Track Presets

Most of us use a similar chain of effects on certain tracks. There is no need to recreate the same effects chains again and again. You can use Track Presets to store your effects chains for future use. Use the following procedure to save your effects chains as Track Presets:

1. In a track, add the chain of effects you want to save (see Figure 6.34).

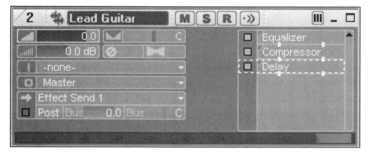

Figure 6.34
An effects chain in a track.

2. In each effect, create the default settings you want to start with when you insert a new track.

3. Right-click on the track and choose Save as a Track Template.

4. In the Export Track Template dialog box, enter a file name and click Save.

Isolating or Removing Drum Hits Using Gating

Using this technique, you can isolate drum hits from a pattern or loop, and in some instances, even remove them.

Although seemingly little more than an open/close switch for audio, gating can be very powerful, especially when you use the side-chaining functionality. Although side-chaining can allow you to trigger a gate with a discreet source, you'll actually be using the same audio source, but processing it to get a more precise gating effect.

There are two ways to achieve this effect—by using side-chaining with a plug-in like the FX Dynamic processor (which uses the left channel as the key signal), or by using a plug-in like the Sonitus Gate, which includes internal processing that allows you to equalize the signal that triggers the gate without affecting the signal that passes through the gate.

1. Patch the Sonitus Gate onto a drum track.

2. Set the Output control to Sidechain. You will now hear the signal that the plug-in is using for triggering the gate. It will be identical to the regular signal until you start adjusting the filters.

3. Play the drum part and use the high and low cut filters to zoom in on a particular drum sound (kick, snare, hi-hat). You should not try to be too exact, because a drum sound will have components across several frequencies.

4. Switch the output mode back to Audio and bring the threshold up until only the sound you focused on is coming through. Now adjust the release and hold to be as short as possible without clicking or cutting off the hit. Attack time should be kept low. See Figure 6.35.

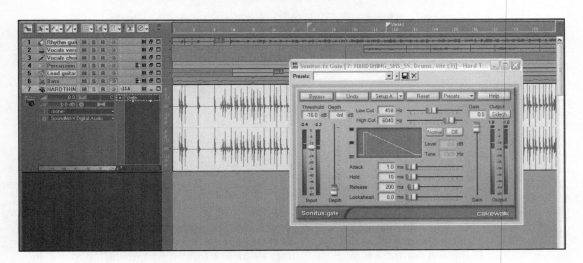

Figure 6.35

Sonitus:fx Gate settings for side-chaining.

To remove only the selected hit, toggle the Normal control to Duck. You will probably need to set a *look ahead time* of about 10-12 ms. You'll notice that removing the signal isn't quite as effective as isolating it—also you'll remove any other sounds that occur at the same time (hi-hats, and so on).

You can achieve even better results by using a more adjustable EQ. To do this, you'll need to copy the original track and hard pan each instance in the opposite direction, and then run them into a new bus using the FX1 Dynamics Processor patched into the bus's FX bin. Then patch an EQ to the track that is hard-panned left. When the FX plug-in is set to Sidechain mode, it will use the left signal as the trigger, although the results will only be mono (see Figure 6.36).

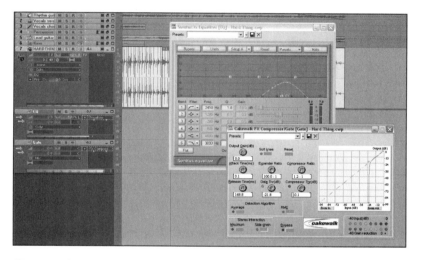

Figure 6.36
FX Compressor/Gate settings for side-chaining.

Synchronizing Sonitus Delay to SONAR's Tempo

When using delay, you'll get the best results when the tempo of your project matches the delayed signal in your plug-in. With synchronization, the delayed signal is in time with your project. Synchronizing delay to match your project's tempo can take some time—but not if you are using Sonitus:fx Delay. To synchronize Sonitus:fx Delay to SONAR's tempo:

1. Insert Sonitus:fx Delay into an effects bin.
2. In the Sonitus:fx Delay's property page, click the Tempo Sync button until it says Host (see Figure 6.37).

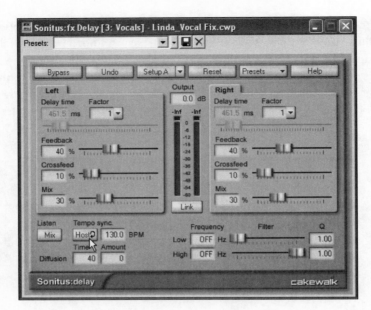

Figure 6.37

The Tempo
Sync button
in Sonitus:fx
Delay.

3. In SONAR, click the Play button. Sonitus:fx Delay automatically syncs up with SONAR.

Restoring the Cancel Button in Effects Property Pages

Cakewalk has dramatically reduced interruptions to playback when editing data or adjusting parameters. These interruptions are often called *gapping*. In their drive to eliminate gapping, the good folks at Cakewalk have had to make a few feature concessions. One handy item that no longer appears in SONAR 5 is the Cancel button in an effect's property page when using an effect offline. The purpose of the Cancel button was to revert the plug-in's settings back to its state when the property page was opened, thereby undoing the changes made to the effect. The Cancel button is now gone by default, but with a simple addition to the Cakewalk.ini file, you can have the Cancel button back. To do so:

1. Navigate to where you installed SONAR 5.

2. Using Notepad or some other text editor, open cakewalk.ini.

3. Add the following line to the [WinCake] section of the cakewalk.ini file:

   EnablePluginCancelButton=1

4. Save the cakewalk.ini file (see Figure 6.38).

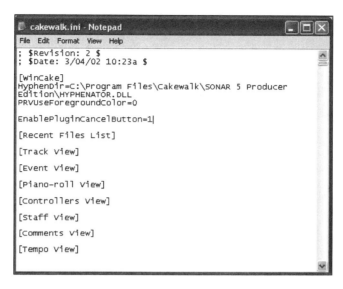

Figure 6.38
The line `EnablePluginCancelButton` in the Cakewalk.ini file.

When you re-open SONAR and patch in an offline effect (select a track or clip and right-click), the Cancel button appears.

If you want to revert back to the SONAR 5 default behavior, simply change the 1 to a 0 (zero).

Fixing Anomalies when Using DXis and Look-Ahead Effects

Some effects use a look-ahead buffer which is eventually compensated for by SONAR's Automatic Delay Compensation (ADC). However, when you are using these effects on the outputs of some virtual instruments, especially at higher latencies, you might experience drop-outs or missed notes from the original MIDI track. This is usually caused because SONAR is not supplying enough MIDI data upstream for ADC. Fortunately, you can increase the MIDI buffer size. To do so:

1. Choose Options > Global from the SONAR menu.
2. In the Global Options dialog box, click on the MIDI tab.
3. In the Playback section, adjust the value in the option: Prepare Using Millisecond Buffers (see Figure 6.39).

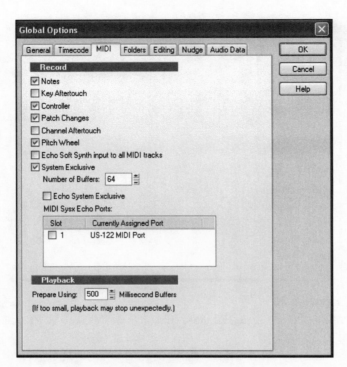

4. The default is 500 ms. Try increasing this value at 100 ms increments until you are satisfied with the performance.

Remapping MIDI Controllers to Automate or Edit Hardware or Software Synthesizers

This tip shows you how to automate or edit the parameters of most hardware and software instruments, using any MIDI controller or keyboard, regardless of the type and value of information that it sends. Even without a control surface, you can still have hands-on control without having to constantly remap controllers.

1. Insert a VST or DXi, or route a MIDI track to the hardware port your keyboard is plugged in to.

2. Open the Track Inspector (press the I key on your keyboard).

3. Show the assignable widgets by clicking the FX button until it is blue (see Figure 6.40).

Figure 6.40

Assignable widgets in the Track Inspector.

4. Right-click on the first widget and choose Reassign Control. The MIDI Parameter Type dialog box will appear (see Figure 6.41).

Most instruments will use a fixed set of MIDI controller values. Most hardware and older software instruments use Continuous Controllers, although more recently, Non-registered Parameter Numbers (NRPNs) are used for the higher resolution they can provide.

If you are using a hardware instrument, consult the manual to see which controls are used for each parameter.

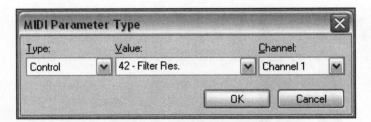

Figure 6.41

MIDI Parameter Type dialog box.

Set the widgets accordingly. Also, be sure to enable the widgets by unchecking the Disable Control option which it, annoyingly, defaults to every time you make a change. Don't worry that only four widgets are visible at a time; in reality, you'll be able to use as many as you need to map controls.

Let's map some controllers:

1. Right-click on the first widget and choose Remote Control.
2. Move the control you want to use. It can be a Mod wheel, knob, slider, even a MIDI note will work, although it produces only two values.
3. Press Learn and you should see the control method reflected in the Remote Control dialog box (see Figure 6.42).

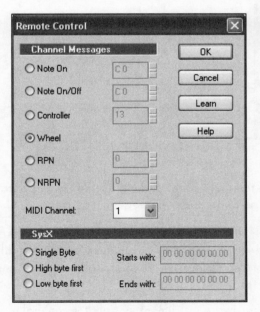

Figure 6.42

The Remote Control dialog box.

4. Repeat for as many controllers as you want. Arm the widgets for automation before reassigning them. Even after you reassign a widget, the Remote Control mapping of that parameter will remain, meaning you're not limited to just four controls.

5. Record automation at any time by using the Record Automation button in the transport.

If you want to control multiple parameters with one physical control, you can use grouping to latch multiple sliders together. Using the Group Manager you can actually set the controls to preserve relative or absolute value to each other, or even invert (see Figure 6.43) their responses. Certain parameters, such as cutoff and resonance or tuning and FM modulation, make good groups because of the interplay needed between them to affect the output signal.

Figure 6.43

Two controls grouped as inverted.

7 Mastering, Collaboration, and Distribution

Making, sharing, and selling music has become easier than ever with broadband making it possible to send large files over long distances. SONAR users can collaborate with other SONAR users, but also with users of different audio applications on other platforms. In just the last few years, faster computers and powerful plug-ins have made desktop mastering a reality for anyone willing to take the time to develop their ears. This chapter covers the final stages of an audio project: the exchange of files for recording and mixing; the mastering of the final mix; and the distribution of the final product to various file formats.

Sharing Files with Others

With the increasing popularity of desktop music production, it is becoming easier to share your work with others, whether they are in the same town or on the other side of the world. The following tips show you how to share your work with others, whether or not they use SONAR.

Preserve Track Timing with Broadcast Waves

Broadcast waves are the same as other wave files, except they have encoded in them a time stamp that tells SONAR exactly where they should be in your project when you import them. Using Broadcast wave files is a simple way to collaborate with other SONAR users or with users of other applications that support broadcast waves. The following procedure shows a typical collaboration using Broadcast wave files:

1. Deliver your project to your collaborator in one of the following ways:

   ❋ A data CD or DVD of your entire project and all its audio—This is the best option if the person you are working with has a system with all the effects and virtual instruments used in the project and his or her machine is fast enough to deal with the processing power needed for the project.

   ❋ A Cakewalk Bundle file—A Bundle contains all the MIDI, automation, and audio data in your project. The audio is uncompressed, but you can reduce the size of a Bundle to make delivery easier. See the tip "Reduce the Size of Bundle Files" that follows for more information on how to do that.

   ❋ A Broadcast wave file mixdown of your project—This is much smaller than the full project and should work just as well under most circumstances.

   ❋ An MP3 mixdown of the project—This method works just fine as long as the timing is preserved by selecting the export from the very beginning of the project (time zero). An MP3 has the obvious advantage of being smaller than a wave file and much smaller than the full project. You can even e-mail an MP3 to most people.

2. Instruct those who receive a wave or MP3 file to import the file into a project in SONAR. If it is an MP3, they should import the file at the very beginning of the project. Broadcast wave files should be allowed to open at their time stamp and should not be moved in time. Collaborators who get a project can simply open it and begin to work on the new track or tracks.

3. The collaborators can create as many new tracks as they need to.
4. When they are finished working on the project, they should export each track separately as a Broadcast wave file (see Figure 7.1).

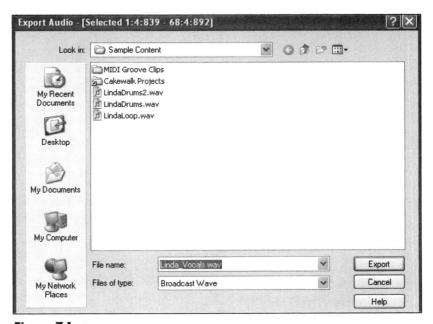

Figure 7.1
The Export dialog box with Broadcast Wave selected as the file type.

5. The resulting files are sent back to you.
6. Open the original project and import each new file.

Export OMF Files

Many audio applications support OMF (Open Media Format), providing a convenient way to share your work with someone who does not use SONAR. Applications that support OMF files include Cubase, Nuendo, Pro Tools, Logic Pro, Final Cut Pro, and Digital Performer. Unfortunately, OMF is limited in its support for audio editing features, so some information about your project will not be included in the exported OMF file. The following is a checklist for preparing your project for export to OMF:

❋ No MIDI—OMF does not support MIDI, so if you need the MIDI tracks in your project, now is the time to mix them down to audio. If you were planning on having your collaborator mix down the MIDI to audio (perhaps they have the sound module you want to use), saving the MIDI in your project as a .mid file might be a solution. You can do this by simply saving your project as a standard MIDI file of either type 0 or 1, because the audio is ignored when you save to that format.

❋ No Video—If your project includes video, you have to send it as a separate file, as SONAR does not include video in an OMF project.

❋ Audio format—You have the option of creating .wav files (PC) or AIFF files (Mac). Find out what platform you are creating the OMF file for and create the appropriate audio file format.

❋ OMF Version—OMF version 1 is for older applications, whereas OMF version 2 is the latest. Ask your collaborators which version they need.

❋ No Effects—If you want to send along your effects, you must mix them down first because OMF does not support effects.

❋ No Automation—If you want your automation preserved, bounce the automated track or tracks down before saving to OMF.

❋ No Volume or Pan settings—In SONAR, your volume and pan settings are not included in the OMF file.

❋ No Tempo information—You can create a MIDI click track that mirrors the tempo map and mix it down to an audio click.

❋ Fades and Crossfades are made permanent—Any fades or crossfades in your project are bounced down, so unless you are absolutely certain you don't want to change any of them, you might want to avoid fades prior to export.

❋ Dual Mono or Stereo—Some target systems might not be able to read stereo interleaved files at higher bit depths. It is safer to check the Split Stereo Tracks into Dual Mono check box in the Export OMF dialog box (see Figure 7.2) if you have any doubts.

The recipients of this project need some information from you if they are going to be mixing this project. It is a good idea to include a README file with detailed instructions along with the OMF file.

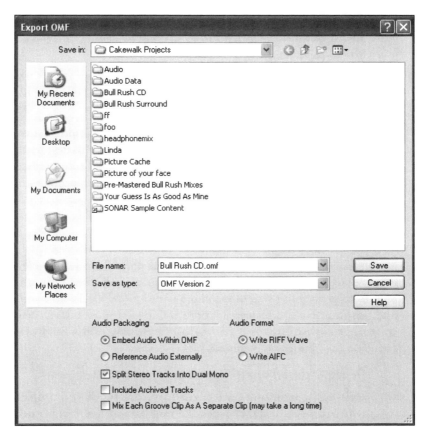

Figure 7.2
The Export OMF dialog box.

Import OMF Files

Collaborating with someone using OMF files requires a little preparation to make sure things go smoothly. SONAR is flexible—it can, for example, import Mac or PC audio files—but in order to work quickly, it is best to instruct the one exporting the OMF file on what settings you prefer. The following is a list of what the OMF file creator should do when exporting the file for you:

✻ Export the file as OMF version 2—SONAR supports both version 1 and version 2, but version 2 is the better choice if available.

✻ Render all pan and volume automation before exporting—SONAR's implementation of OMF does not support these.

❋ Save the audio as wave files—SONAR supports the AIFF file format, but AIFF files must be converted to wave files when the file is opened, which is time-consuming.

❋ Read the application's documentation about exporting OMFs—Every application handles OMF export differently, and it is best to know sooner, rather than later, what those differences are.

❋ Include a text file of instructions—This text file should include information about tempo, pan and volume settings, additional files that need to be imported, and so on. Such information makes it possible to closely replicate the original application's version of the project and reduces the likelihood of having to do things over.

Reduce the Size of Bundle Files

Bundle files are not compressed, so if your project—including all its audio—is large, your Bundle file is going to be large as well. There are a few things you can do to reduce the size of a Bundle file to make it easier to share with others, and perhaps even to squeeze it onto a CD instead of a DVD. **Make a copy of your original project file** before using any of the following tips for reducing the size of your Bundle file:

❋ Delete archived tracks if you aren't going to use them.

❋ Delete any unnecessary tracks. If you are sending a project to someone who is adding a guitar track, he might need the drums and bass, but probably not the shaker or harmony vocals. Only keep the tracks that are necessary.

❋ Use the Remove Silence command or slice out unwanted sections of audio by hand, and then use the Apply Trimming command to remove those sections permanently. See Figure 7.3 for an example of a track with the Remove Silence and Apply Trimming commands applied.

Once you have eliminated the unnecessary parts in your project, you can save the project as a Bundle file.

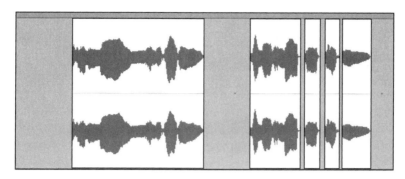

Figure 7.3

A track after the Remove Silence and Apply Trimming commands have been applied.

Using Markers to Make an Exact Export Selection

There are a lot of ways to make an export selection in SONAR. You can make a selection in the Time Ruler, lasso a bunch of clips, or select the tracks. Sometimes, especially when you are trying to make a very precise export, these methods are too cumbersome. There is a simple way to make an exact export selection using markers and the snap grid. Here's how:

1. Turn off Snap to Grid by clicking the Snap to Grid button in the Track view.

2. Find the exact beginning of what you want to export, zooming in if necessary.

3. Add a marker at that location, giving it a descriptive name (see Figure 7.4).

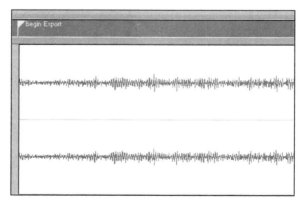

Figure 7.4

Beginning marker.

4. Repeat steps 2 and 3 at the end of what you want to export.

5. Click the drop-down menu in the Snap to Grid button to open the Snap To Grid dialog box.

6. In the Snap To Grid dialog box, click the Markers radio button (see Figure 7.5).

Figure 7.5

The Snap To Grid dialog box with Markers selected.

7. Click the Snap to Grid button to enable Snap to Grid.

8. Click in the Time Ruler near the marker. The initial click needs to be closer to that marker than any other for it to snap to that marker.

9. Drag along the Time Ruler and release the mouse button when you are near the end marker.

10. The selection automatically snaps to the two markers you created (see Figure 7.6).

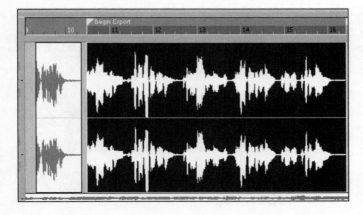

Figure 7.6

A marker to marker selection.

Using Per-Project Audio

The easiest way to collaborate with another SONAR user is to use per-project audio, which keeps all the audio files in a subfolder of the project, and burn the entire folder and the audio subfolder onto a DVD or CD, or save it to an external hard drive. Even if your project was not created with its own audio folder, you can make it a per-project audio project by using the Save As command and, in the Project Path field at the bottom of the Save As dialog box, adding the folder where you want to save the file. If the folder does not exist, you are asked if you want it to be created. After you click Yes, you will see that the Audio Path is set to a subfolder of the new folder your created.

There are a few potential pitfalls when sharing entire projects. The following tips can help to minimize any problems when collaborating:

* Upon receipt of any edits from the other party, make a new copy of the project with some kind of distinctive suffix, such as the date and their initials. This makes it much easier to trace any problems that might arise.

* All systems that share the same project should make sure they have the same effects or any other third-party plug-ins or instruments installed. Synching presets is a good idea as well. See the set of topics under the heading "Synchronizing Presets Between Multiple Workstations" that follows.

* Archive all original audio files in case of file corruption.

Overcoming Name Size Limit in Pro Tools

Pro Tools, and some other audio applications, will not allow you to import files with 32 or more characters in the name. Because of SONAR's naming scheme, you'll often find that the contents of the audio folder easily exceed 32 characters. Although renaming is an option, it can be time-consuming when dealing with many clips.

Jim Willsher has created a powerful, easy-to-use Bulk Rename Utility that's available for free from www.bulkrenameutility.co.uk. See Figure 7.7.

After exporting your wav, aiff, or BWFs, launch Bulk Rename Utility (BRU) and point it to the folder containing your newly exported audio.

1. Select all the files you've just exported by pressing Ctrl+A.
2. Under the Selection field, set the Name Len Min to 30. This way, you won't see or have to rename files that are compliant.

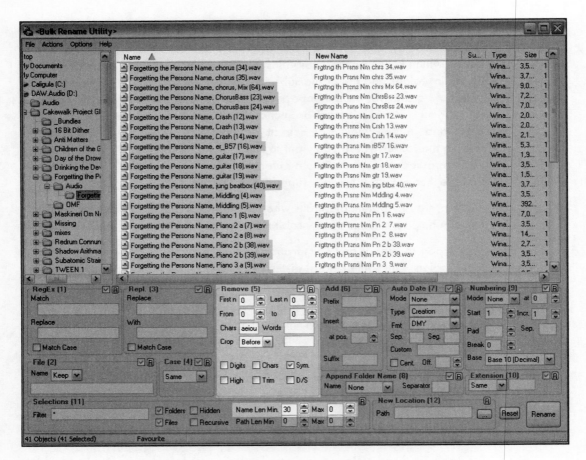

Figure 7.7

The Bulk Rename Utility.

3. Under the Remove field, enter **aeiou** under Chars. Removing the vowels from the file names is a quick way to shorten the names while still retaining legibility (see Figure 7.8).

4. If they are *still* too long, you can remove parentheses and underscores by checking the Sym. box under remove.

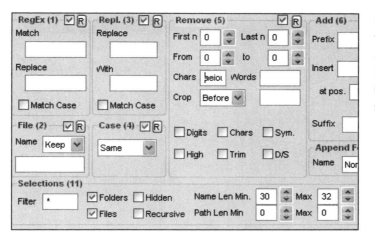

Figure 7.8
The lower-left section of the Bulk Rename Utility showing the fields mentioned in the above steps.

Collaborating on a Mix via E-Mail

Once all collaborators have all the project's audio, or if the project consists of just MIDI data and virtual instruments, sharing files over e-mail becomes a practical and efficient way of working together. Project files (extension: .cwp) contain all of a project's MIDI data, yet they are comparatively small files. As long as everyone has the same effects and virtual instruments installed, all parties can send updated project files back and forth.

Synchronizing Presets Between Multiple Workstations

If you have spent the time to create a number of effects presets and you want to share them with others or move them to a machine, you need only copy the appropriate Registry key and import it to another machine. The following three tips deal with exporting and importing presets.

Exporting and Importing Effects Presets

You can export Mixdown and Bouncing to Tracks presets from the Registry of one machine and import them into the Registry of another. To do so:

1. Click the Start button and choose Run from the Start menu.
2. Type **regedit** in the Run field and press Enter. The Registry Editor opens.
3. Click the plus arrow next to HKEY_CURRENT_USER to expand the category (see Figure 7.9).

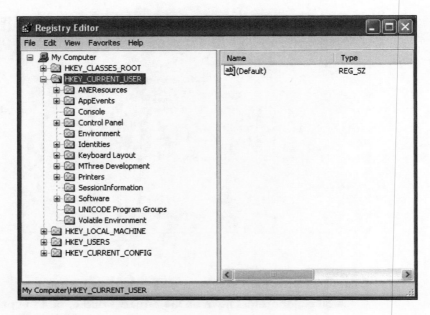

Figure 7.9

Expand a Registry category by clicking the plus sign next to it.

4. Do the same to expand Software, Cakewalk Music Software, either SONAR Producer or SONAR Studio, 5.0, and Presets.

5. Click on Presets. You should see something like what you see in Figure 7.10.

6. Click on the following key:

   FD3918AE-AF3D-414B-8701-C9A02623E875}

7. In the Registry Editor menu, choose File > Export.

8. In the Export Registry File dialog box, enter a name for the Registry file. This is just a partial Registry export, based on the selection you have made.

Once you have saved the .reg file you have created, you can e-mail it to another machine or save it to any portable media (CD-R, floppy disc, and so on) and import it into another machine's Registry. To import the Registry file you have exported:

1. Open the Registry Editor, as described previously.

2. Choose File > Import from the menu.

3. In the Import Registry File dialog box, navigate to and select the .reg file you want to import and click OK.

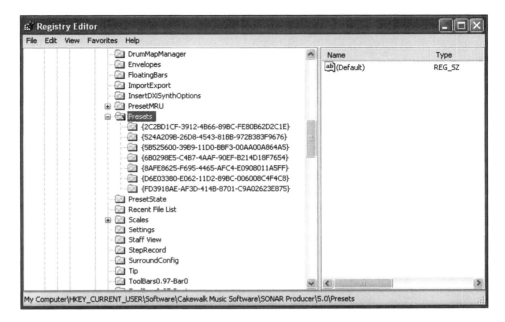

Figure 7.10
The Presets Registry setting displayed.

Exporting and Importing Custom Scales

If you have created any custom scales, you don't have to recreate them on a new machine. Instead, you can export them from your Registry and import them on the new machine. To do so:

1. Click the Start button and choose Run from the Start menu.
2. Type **regedit** in the Run field and press Enter. The Registry Editor opens.
3. Click the plus arrow next to HKEY_CURRENT_USER to expand the category.
4. Do the same to expand Software, Cakewalk Music Software, either SONAR Producer or SONAR Studio, 5.0, and Scales.
5. Click on Scales. You should see something like what you see in Figure 7.11.

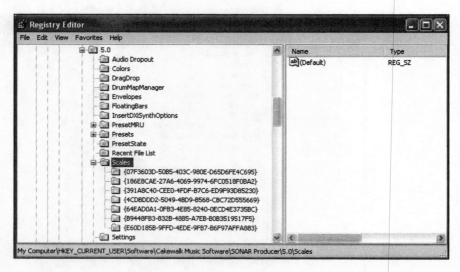

Figure 7.11

The Scales Registry setting displayed.

6. Click on the following key:

   {E60D185B-9FFD-4EDE-9FB7-B6F97AFFA883}

7. In the Registry Editor menu, choose File > Export.

8. In the Export Registry File dialog box, enter a name for the Registry file. This is just a partial Registry export, based on the selection you have made.

Once you have saved the .reg file you have created, you can e-mail it to another machine or save it to any portable media (CD-R, floppy disc, and so on) and import it into another machine's Registry. To import the Registry file you have exported:

1. Open the Registry Editor, as described previously.

2. Choose File > Import from the menu.

3. In the Import Registry File dialog box, navigate to and select the .reg file you want to import and click OK.

Exporting and Importing Color Presets

You can export all of your color presets from the Registry and import them into the Registry of another. To do so:

1. Click the Start button and choose Run from the Start menu.
2. Type **regedit** in the Run field and press Enter. The Registry Editor opens.
3. Click the plus arrow next to HKEY_CURRENT_USER to expand the category.
4. Do the same to expand Software, Cakewalk Music Software, either SONAR Producer or SONAR Studio, 5.0, and Presets.
5. Click on the following key:

   {6B0298E5-C4B7-4AAF-90EF-B214D18F7654}

   You should see something like what you see in Figure 7.12.

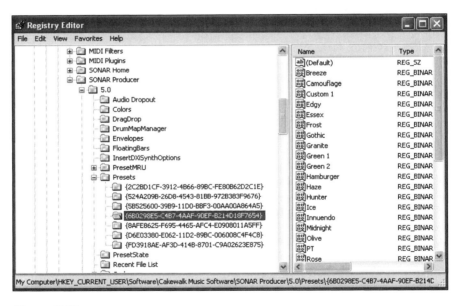

Figure 7.12

The Colors Registry setting displayed.

6. In the Registry Editor menu, choose File > Export.
7. In the Export Registry File dialog box, enter a name for the Registry file. This is just a partial Registry export, based on the selection you have made.

Once you have saved the .reg file you have created, you can e-mail it to another machine, or save it to any portable media (CD-R, floppy disc, and so on) and import it into another machine's Registry. To import the Registry file you have exported:

1. Open the Registry Editor, as described previously.
2. Choose File > Import from the menu.
3. In the Import Registry File dialog box, navigate to and select the .reg file you want to import and click OK.

Configuring SONAR to Use Third-Party Encoders

Out of the box, SONAR allows you to export your projects to .wav, .wma, and .mp3 (for a limited time). The are other formats, including Ogg Vorbis and FLAC, that have gained some followers. The following three tips deal with using SONAR with several third-party encoders.

Configuring MP3 Encoders

There are several free MP3 encoders out there, but if you have downloaded and installed Audacity as described in Chapter 1's section called "Adding Applications to the Tools Menu," you already have an excellent MP3 encoder available. To use Audacity as an MP3 encoder:

1. If you have not already done so, add Audacity to SONAR's Tools menu. See Chapter 1 for details.
2. If you have effects you want included in the MP3, use the Freeze command on the track to include them.
3. Select a track you want to convert to an MP3.
4. Choose Tools > Audacity from the SONAR menu.
5. Audacity opens the .wav file you had selected. See Figure 7.13.
6. If you want, you can make changes to the file; for example, dither it down to 16-bit.
7. In Audacity, choose File > Export as MP3.
8. In the Save MP3 File As dialog box, enter a file name and navigate to the directory where you want to save the file. Click Save.
9. Enter your song's information in the ID3 Tags dialog box and click OK.

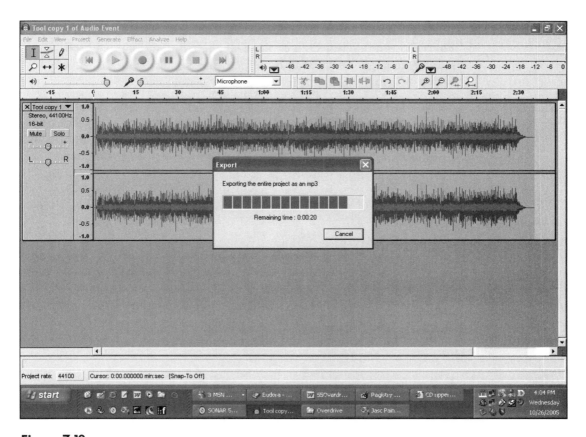

Figure 7.13

Wave file being exported to an MP3 in Audacity.

Configuring Ogg Vorbis Encoders

Ogg Vorbis is a free, open-source codec that is growing in popularity. There are several variations of the Ogg Vorbis encoder available. Once you have installed an encoder, you can add it to the Tools menu in SONAR. This example uses the oggdropXPd encoder. Visit www.vorbis.com for a list of links to Ogg Vorbis encoders you can use. The following procedure shows you how to use the Ogg Vorbis encoder oggdropXPd in SONAR:

1. Install the Ogg Vorbis encoder you have downloaded and add it to your Tools menu. For instructions on how to do that, see the topic "Adding Applications to the Tools Menu" in Chapter 1.

2. In SONAR, open a project that has the audio you want to mix down.

3. Bounce down the project to a stereo track. If you are at the mastering stage, you might be creating an Ogg Vorbis file along with a wave file for creating a CD master.

4. If you want, you can add fade-ins and fade-outs to the stereo track.

5. If you want your Ogg Vorbis file to have a specific name, right-click on the stereo track and choose Properties from the menu that appears to open the Clip Properties dialog box and enter a name for the track.

6. Choose the encoder from the Tools menu.

7. oggdropPXd opens (see Figure 7.14).

Figure 7.14

The oggdropPXd interface.

8. Right-click anywhere on the interface to view the menu where you can customize the output of the file in the following ways:

   ❊ Select Output Directory—Set the default output directory (see Figure 7.15).

   ❊ Encoding Options—Set the quality of the output file (see Figure 7.16).

9. Drag your stereo file onto the interface.

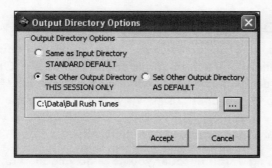

Figure 7.15

The oggdrdopPXd Select Output Directory dialog box.

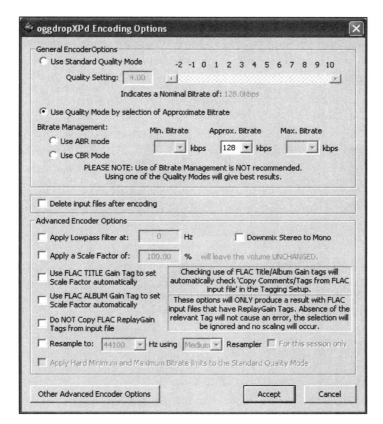

Figure 7.16

The oggdrdopPXd Encoding Options dialog box.

Configuring FLAC Encoders

FLAC (Free Lossless Audio Codec) is, as you might guess, a lossless audio compression codec. FLAC is supported by a growing list of companies, including RIO portable players and several car stereo manufacturers. Several big-name artists offer FLAC files as downloads. Although bigger than MP3s, FLAC files are lossless, so when converted to wave files, they are identical to the CD they came from. To use the FLAC encoder with SONAR, follow this procedure:

1. Download the FLAC encoder (from http://flac.sourceforge.net) and install it.

2. Add the FLAC encoder to the Tools menu. For instructions on how to do that, see the topic "Adding Applications to the Tools Menu" in Chapter 1.

3. In SONAR, open a project that has the audio you want to mix down.

4. Bounce down the project to a stereo track.

5. If you want, you can add fade-ins and fade-outs to the stereo track.

6. If you want your FLAC file to have a specific name, right-click on the stereo track and choose Properties from the menu that appears. The Clip Properties dialog box opens, where you can name the track.

7. Choose the FLAC frontend from the Tools menu. Figure 7.17 shows FLAC frontend's interface.

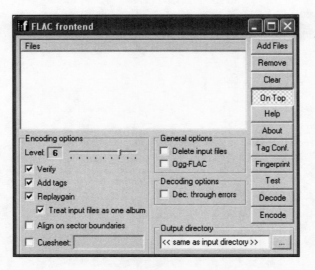

Figure 7.17

The FLAC frontend interface.

8. Drag the stereo track onto the FLAC frontend interface.

9. Click the On Top button to keep the interface on top of SONAR (see Figure 7.18).

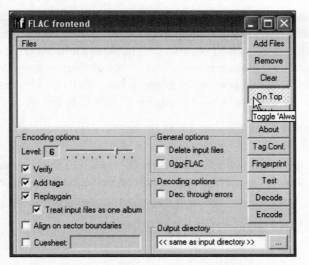

Figure 7.18

The Always on Top button in FLAC.

10. In the FLAC frontend interface, customize the output of the file in the following ways:

   ✻ Encoding Options—Set the quality of the output file using the Level slider.

   ✻ Output Directory—Set the output directory.

11. Drag your stereo file into the Files field.
12. Click Encode.

Mastering a CD in SONAR

SONAR isn't just for recording and editing audio and MIDI. You can use SONAR to master a project. It has all the tools you need to get excellent results. The following tips are about using SONAR to master a CD.

Setting Up a Mastering Project

You begin by creating a new project and customizing it for your project.

1. If you have not already created a mastering template, you can start with the template 16 Tracks Audio.
2. Add tracks, if necessary, until you have one for each track going on the CD.
3. Import tracks in the order they will appear on the CD. The tracks should not overlap; each track should be later in time than the previous track. Figure 7.19 shows how this should look.

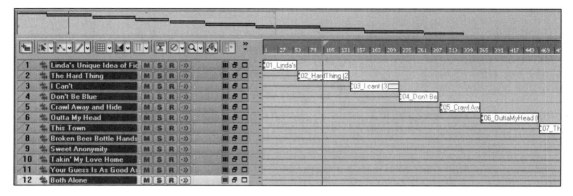

Figure 7.19

A typical mastering project's track layout.

4. Create a Main bus and add a limiter.

5. Add two instances of an EQ and a compressor plug-in to each track (see Figure 7.20). You want to use an EQ with multiple bands and variable Q, like the Sonitus:fx EQ included with SONAR.

Figure 7.20
EQ and Compressor plug-in each track.

6. Take the time now to create a template of your project and a Track Preset from one of the tracks.

7. Save your project.

Adding Fades

Before you begin listening to the same track over and over, you can get rid of the silence before and after the track and add your fade-ins and fade outs. First, you set the beginning and end of the track, and then you add the fades.

1. Slip-edit the beginning and end of each tune right up to the instant there is a signal.

2. If you want to use a fade-in or fade-out on a track, drag one out using your mouse, like in Figure 7.21.

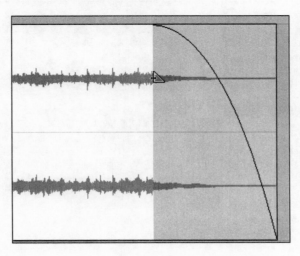

Figure 7.21
Dragging out a fade-out on a track.

3. If necessary, right-click on the fade to change the type, like in Figure 7.22.

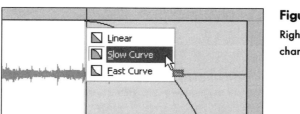

Figure 7.22

Right-click on a fade-out to change the fade type.

4. Listen to the fades to determine whether they sound good in the context of the song and shorten or lengthen them accordingly.

Adding Corrective EQ

First, you need to fix any problems you hear in each track. You'll do this using EQ.

1. Solo the track you are working on.

2. Open the first EQ's property page. For this example, you'll use the Sonitus:fx EQ.

3. In one of the bands, set the Q to its highest setting which, in the case of the Sonitus:fx EQ, is 24.

4. Raise the level of the band to about +10dB.

5. Select and slowly drag the band back and forth while listening to the track. You are listening for any unpleasant or annoying sounds. Once you have found a sound you don't like, lower the level of the band below unity to perhaps -3 or -4dB. If you find you want to cut more than this, chances are there are problems in the mix and it can be best fixed on individual tracks rather than the stereo mixdown.

6. Use the Bypass button in Sonitus:fx EQ to compare the original sound and the sound with EQ.

7. Repeat these steps, using other bands, until you don't hear anything that bothers you. See Figure 7.23 for an example of corrective EQ.

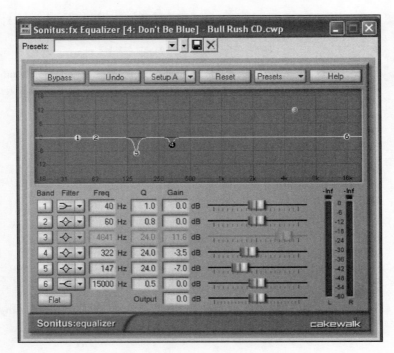

Figure 7.23

Corrective EQ
in Sonitus:fx
Equalizer.

Using EQ to Sweeten and Balance

Now is a good time to take a step back and compare the tracks you are working on to tracks on some of your favorite CDs. Collect a handful of CDs that
are in the same genre as the project you are working on. Listen to those CDs,
and then listen to the tracks you are mastering. You are listening for the amount
of bass, mids, and treble in each track. Once you know what you want to add
to your project, do the following:

1. Open the property page for the second EQ.

2. Add EQ according to what you heard when A/Bing your mix with other
   CDs. The following is a list of common balancing and sweetening EQ:

   ❋ Bass boost—Use a very low Q setting to create a 1 or 2dB boost in
     the bass frequencies.

   ❋ Mids boost or cut—Use a very low Q setting to create a 1 or 2dB
     boost or cut in the mids.

   ❋ Add shimmer—Use a low Q setting to add 1 or 2dB to the frequencies
     above 10kHz.

See Figure 7.24 for an example of sweetening EQ.

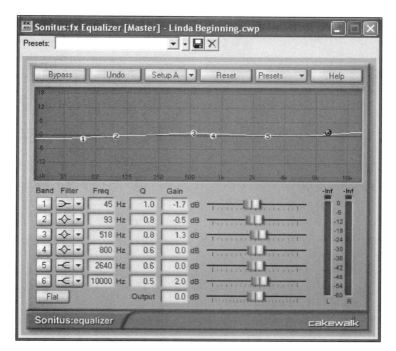

Figure 7.24

An example of sweetening EQ in Sonitus:fx Equalizer.

Add Compression

Perhaps the most overused effect during mastering is compression. The trend in recent years is to make everything sound loud, which sounds great—at least until your ears get fatigued. Of course, you almost always can use some compression on a mix, so let's add some:

1. Open the compression plug-in you added to each track.

2. Set the knee to soft for more transparent compression or hard for more aggressive compression.

3. Play back the track soloed and adjust the threshold until the Gain Reduction meter (GR) hits a maximum of about 6dB. Tweak it from there to find a setting you like. This process might take many listens and breaks.

4. Adjust the Gain level in the EQ until you are close to clipping in the track. See Figure 7.25 for typical mastering compression settings in Sonitus:fx Compressor.

Figure 7.25
Typical settings for the Sonitus:fx
Compressor when mastering.

Level Matching

Mastering is about adding the final polish and consistency, and level matching
is one of the most important parts of consistency. If you listen to a CD, you
don't have to get up and change the volume after every song! To match levels:

1. In each track, beginning with the "louder" songs, adjust the Volume
   fader so that the Limiter is kicking in on the Main bus.

2. In the softer songs, which have fewer instruments and a more intimate
   feel (ballads for example), make sure that the overall volume is less than
   the louder songs.

3. Listen to each track back to back in order and tweak the volumes until
   you feel they are consistent.

Adding Reverb

In general, you shouldn't have to add any reverb, but if the mixes are too dry,
and the dryness is not an effect itself, you can add the same reverb to the
tunes at different levels. You can add reverb to some or all of your mixes for
one or more of the following reasons:

❀ Overly dry mixes.

❀ Not much stereo separation—You can use a stereo reverb to add some
   imaging to the tune.

Be careful of these "don'ts" when adding reverb when mastering:

✳ Don't use a reverb that isn't true stereo, as you might hurt the track's stereo image.

✳ Don't use reverb on a track that uses dryness to be more "in your face."

✳ Don't overdo it! Reverb at this stage should be mild and transparent.

To add reverb to your tracks:

1. Create a bus and patch a reverb into it.
2. Open the reverb's property page and adjust its settings for a short reverb; nothing longer than medium room, for example.
3. In each track you want to add reverb to, create a send to the reverb's bus.
4. Adjust the levels in the send. This is the part that requires good ears. In general, if you can hear it, you have overdone it.

Limiter Settings

Your limiter is a guard against digital clipping—something you definitely want to avoid, as you push the volume of each track. The limiter is in the Main bus to prevent the peak transients from exceeding 0dB. With that in mind, use the following guidelines when setting your limiter:

✳ Use a hard limit setting—The limiter parameters should be such that no signal exceeds 0dB.

✳ Use a "look ahead" feature if available.

✳ Set the attack to the smallest number possible to prevent any transients rising above 0dB.

✳ If your limiter has a built-in dithering option, you can use it, but if you do, make sure you turn off the SONAR dithering so you are not doing it twice.

Exporting Mastered Files

When you are done and ready to mix down your tracks to 16-bit versions, use the following checklist:

✳ Make sure you are dithering just once. If your limiter has a dithering option, and you prefer it, make sure SONAR's dithering is off in the Advanced tab of the Audio Options dialog box. If you are using SONAR's dithering, make sure it is set to the best quality: POW-r 3.

❋ If you are exporting the project track by track, mute all but the track you are exporting. You can do this quickly by clicking the M button in the Playback State toolbar, and then unmuting the one track you are exporting.

❋ Select the track you are exporting. Selecting the track ensures that you are exporting only that track without any extra time selection.

❋ Open the Audio Options dialog box, and on the General tab, check the 64-bit Double Precision Engine check box (see Figure 7.26).

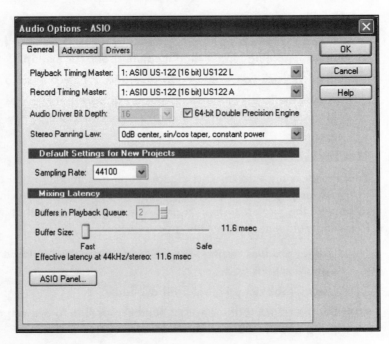

Figure 7.26

The 64-bit Double Precision Engine option in the Audio Options dialog box.

Now you can export your project as individual tracks or as one long file. You make this decision based on what software you are going to use to create the final CD. If you want to create custom fades between songs, for example, you might want to get into the details of Red Book Audio codes. If so, you should create a single file and add codes to it. Most often, you create individual files and use a product like Nero or Cakewalk's Media Works and adjust the gaps between songs as desired.

Setting Up SONAR to Use Analog Summing

Although most people are inclined to mix relying only on software effects, EQ, and summing algorithms, creating a final mix using outboard gear and mixers can be a useful technique that brings your sound *out of the box* in more ways than one.

First, SONAR 5 has a new 64-bit double precision audio engine that should remove any doubts that mixing down in the digital domain can give you very high-quality results. You can rest assured that no new noise will be introduced into the mix, and, of course, all of the mixing and bounces can happen faster than real-time.

Conversely, using a multi-output sound card and an external mixer, at the very least to sum the signals, not only gives you a different sound, but gives a new outlook to your song. The latter is the simple part; freeing yourself of an abundance of meters, using somewhat vaguely marked knobs and faders, and not having to stare at a screen will, quite simply, force you to use your ears.

As for the former, there's quite a bit more to it. Although digital summing has reached a state of incredible accuracy, some people might want the elusive *warmth* of analog equipment (an enigmatic mix of distortion and noise). If you are the lucky owner of a Neve or Studer desk, you will find that the EQs you have access to will impart a special quality. If you have a more standard low- or mid-range board, you will be best served by using software processing and merely using the mixer's bus to sum your various subgroups.

To begin, you'll need a sound card with multiple outputs, 8 to 16 channels will prove to be the most useful. Using fewer than 8 requires that you sum many of your busses in the computer anyway, giving you limited flexibility when using the outboard gear. More than 16 channels requires a fairly large mixer, although the results certainly won't suffer.

Your mixer will need an equal number of inputs; however, it is not necessary that they are all full channel strips. Many older mixers feature tape returns that are limited to volume/pan and many current mixers feature line-level inputs with nothing more than a gain control. Some multiple bus mixers allow you to input signals directly to a bus and then route the output to a final stereo pair.

To set up SONAR and your project for analog summing:

1. First, you should create a new bus for each hardware output or output pair. You might want to create two to four mono busses and make the balance stereo. For mono busses, you'll want to make sure the bus is set to Mono and hard panned left or right (outputs have to be selected as stereo pairs).

2. Now insert and activate a send on each bus, sending a signal to a stereo master bus. This allows you to listen to the full mix directly from the computer—useful for reference or A/Bing against the analog summed version.

3. Route your tracks, or preferably, instrument subgroups, to your new busses. Vocals and Bass can use mono busses.

4. Run the master output bus to your mixer, either through a separate set of outputs or through a stereo pair used by another bus. If you do the latter, mute the master bus.

5. Group the solo button on all of the new busses, including the master bus.

6. Open the Group Manager and invert the response of the master bus solo by selecting Custom, and then swapping the start and end value (see Figure 7.27).

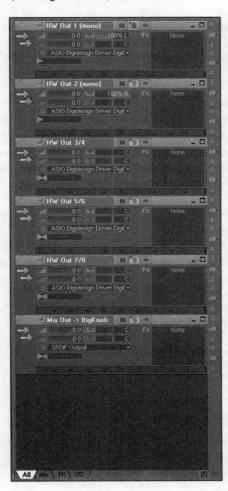

Figure 7.27

Busses in SONAR set up according to the procedure.

To set up your mixer:

1. Route the mono busses from SONAR into channels with pan controls on your mixer. Make sure each output is panned center.

2. If you're running stereo busses into channel pairs on the mixer, make sure to hard pan each channel.

3. Route all of your channels/inputs to a main output bus.

4. Turn down any channels, aux returns, or effects returns that you are not using; they will only add to the noise floor.

5. Put all of your active faders at 0dB.

There is a bit more work with hardware, as you'll be reminded, so the fewer times you need to go back and repeat the process, the better. With that in mind, ask yourself if you can't get results that are as good using plug-ins (or even DSP-powered cards like Universal Audio's UAD-1).

Now you should be all set to go. Your panning and volume are controlled via the software, so resist complicating things by adjusting gain on your outboard mixer as well. You can easily A/B your mix because you grouped your Bus solo buttons. Adjust the volumes so that they are about the same—you can easily convince yourself that one mix is better than another based on volume alone.

Use Presets to Save Mixdown and Bounce Settings

SONAR now has presets for both bouncing down and exporting audio. Presets are a way to instantly repeat previously used settings, ensuring you consistently mixdown accurately. These presets are shared between the Export Audio and Bounce to Tracks dialog boxes. Use the following procedure to create a mixdown or bounce preset:

1. Make an Audio selection.

2. Choose File > Export or Edit > Bounce to Track(s) from the SONAR menu. Figures 7.28 and 7.29 show the Export and Bounce to Track(s) dialog boxes.

Figure 7.28

The Export dialog box.

3. Make your selections in the following categories:

* Source Category

* Channel Format

* Mix Enables options

* Destination—Bounce to Track(s) dialog box only. Categories not included in both dialog boxes are ignored when used in the other.

* Sampling Rate—Export Audio dialog box only

* Bit Depth—Export Audio dialog box only

Figure 7.29
The Bounce to Track(s) dialog box.

4. Enter a name for your preset in the Preset field.

5. Click the Save button to the right of the Preset field to save it.

You can recall presets using the Preset drop-down menu.

8 Video and Surround

SONAR continues to add new video functionality and its implementation of surround sound has been recognized as one of the best among its peer applications. The tips in this chapter help you get the most out of each of those features and your machine.

Setting Up Your 5.1 Speakers

Mixing in surround is more complicated than mixing in stereo. In order for your surround mixes to accurately reflect how they will sound on other systems, you need to place six speakers in appropriate positions. The following is a list of guidelines for placing your speakers for an accurate 5.1 mix.

- All speakers should be equal distances from the mixer (you).
- The center speaker should be directly in front of you.
- The left speaker should be 30 degrees left of center.
- The right speaker should be 30 degrees right of center.
- The left surround speaker (left rear) should be 110 degrees left of center.
- The right surround speaker (right rear) should be 110 degrees right of center.
- The LFE speaker (sub-woofer) doesn't have a specific location.

Figure 8.1 shows how your 5.1 surround speaker setup should look.

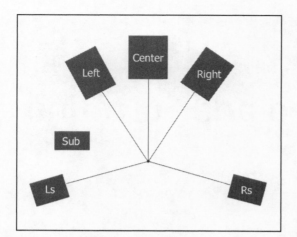

Figure 8.1

5.1 surround speaker arrangement.

Calibrating 5.1 Surround Speaker Levels

Mixing in surround is more than just having five speakers and a sub-woofer. You must make sure the speakers are set up properly, as shown in Figure 8.1, and you must also make sure that your speaker levels are equal. If you don't do this, your mixes won't be accurate and will sound the way you intend them to sound only on your system. Fortunately, calibrating your speakers is not hard. The next two tips show you two different ways to do it.

Using a dB Meter

Once you have set up your speakers according to the previous tip "Setting Up Your 5.1 Speakers," you can use a dB meter and a wave file of "pink noise" to calibrate their levels. Follow this procedure:

1. In SONAR, create a project and import a "pink noise" wave file. Pink noise is a special test signal that has all octaves at equal levels. You can find a free pink noise file on the Internet with a quick search.

2. At the sweet spot (where your head will be), set up the dB meter so it is pointing at the center speaker. dB meters give you an accurate gauge of decibel level. They can be found in both analog and digital models at electronic stores like Radio Shack. If you don't have a dB meter, you can still calibrate your speakers using a microphone. To do so, see the next tip.

3. Play the pink noise file through each speaker individually and note the levels.

4. In the speaker's amplifier, or on the speaker itself, adjust the volume of each of the front three speakers so that they read the same on the dB meter. It is important to keep the following in mind while adjusting levels:

   ❋ You don't want to change the levels once you have them set because this would require you to recalibrate the rest of your speakers, so make sure you are setting the levels for sufficient volume.

   ❋ You want to be able to control your speakers as a group, using a mixer or via the Main Surround Bus in SONAR.

5. Once you've set the levels for the front three speakers, it is time to set the rear surround speakers. You will do the left one first, so turn the dB meter so that it is facing directly left (90 degrees from the center speaker, not directly at the speaker).

6. Play back the pink noise file through the left surround speaker and adjust the volume of that speaker until it matches the ones in front.

7. Turn the dB meter so that it faces directly to the right (90 degrees from center) and set the levels for that speaker.

8. Set the level for the sub-woofer 4dB higher than the other speakers.

9. Adjust the volume of all speakers using your mixer or SONAR's Main Surround Bus.

Using a Microphone

If you don't have a dB meter, you can calibrate your speakers using a quality condenser microphone and a pink noise wave file, as follows:

1. In SONAR, create a project and import a "pink noise" wave file.

2. At the sweet spot (where your head will be), set up a good condenser microphone that has a more or less flat frequency response.

3. Connect the microphone to your sound card.

4. Create a track and set the input to the one connected to your microphone.

5. Arm the track. *Set the output to None.* You don't want to hear the input of the microphone. Doing so would create a feedback loop that can potentially damage your speakers.

6. Record the pink noise file through each speaker individually and play the clip, noting the peak level.

7. In the speaker's amplifier, or on the speaker itself, adjust the volume of each so that the peak level is the same. It is important to keep the following in mind while adjusting levels:

❄ You don't want to change the levels once you have them set because this would require you to recalibrate the rest of your speakers, so make sure you are setting the levels for sufficient volume.

❄ You want to be able to control your speakers as a group, using a mixer or via the Main Surround Bus in SONAR.

8. Once you've set the levels for the front three speakers, it is time to set the rear surround speakers. You will do the left one first, so turn the microphone so that it is facing directly left (90 degrees from the center speaker, not directly at the speaker).

9. Play back the pink noise file through the left surround speaker and adjust the volume of that speaker until it matches the ones in front.

10. Turn the microphone so that it faces directly to the right (90 degrees from center) and set the levels for that speaker.

11. Set the level for the sub-woofer 4dB higher than the other speakers. If your microphone has a dip in the lower frequencies (under 125Hz), you should compensate for this by boosting your sub-woofer volume on top of the additional 4dB you have already added. Consult your microphone's documentation for its frequency response.

Using Stereo or Mono Plug-ins in Your Surround Project

SONAR's SurroundBridge technology lets you use any plug-in in a surround project no matter how many channels there are. To use SurroundBridge:

1. In a surround bus, right-click in the FX field.

2. Select a stereo effect from the menu. SurroundBridge opens with enough instances of plug-in for each channel. See Figure 8.2.

3. Modify the settings in each pair as you would for a single stereo instance.

4. Click the SurroundBridge tab, where you can do the following:

❄ Configure channel pairings

❄ Enable/disable plug-in instances

❄ Unlink instances from automatable parameters

To see the SurroundBridge tab's controls, check out Figure 8.3.

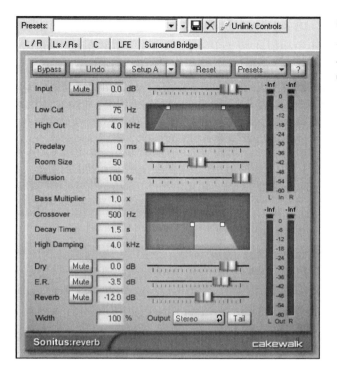

Figure 8.2

Sonitus:fx Reverb in a
5.1 surround project
using SurroundBridge.

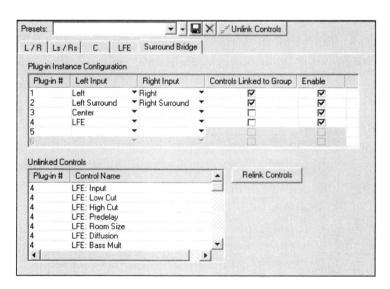

Figure 8.3

SurroundBridge tab controls.

Checking Your Surround Mix in Stereo

SONAR's downmixing option lets you listen to and configure how your surround project sounds in stereo, an important consideration because many listeners will hear your work on a stereo system and not a surround speaker setup. Downmixing works by summing all your surround channels together, at a reduced level, and then splitting the signal between the two stereo channels. Follow this procedure to use downmixing:

1. In your surround project, create a stereo bus.
2. Assign your surround bus outputs to the new stereo bus (see Figure 8.4).

Figure 8.4

A surround bus routed to a stereo bus.

3. Choose Options > Project to open the Project Options dialog box.
4. In the Project Options dialog box, click the Surround tab (see Figure 8.5).

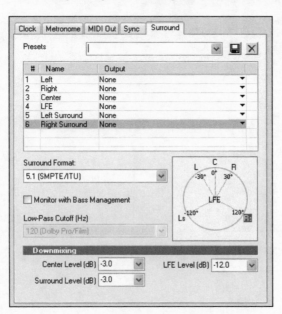

Figure 8.5

The Surround tab in the Project Options dialog box.

5. In the Downmixing section, select an option for the Center Level. This is how SONAR handles the center channel. Select from the following options in the drop-down menu:

   ❋ -3dB

   ❋ -4.5dB

   ❋ -6dB

   ❋ -INF—No signal from the center channel is mixed down in stereo

   ❋ Or enter a custom value

6. In the Downmixing section, select an option for the Surround Level. This is how SONAR handles the left and right surround channels. Select from the following options in the drop-down menu:

   ❋ -3dB

   ❋ -6dB

   ❋ -INF—no signal from the left or right surround channel is mixed down in stereo

   ❋ Or enter a custom value

7. In the Downmixing section, select an option for the LFE Level. This is how SONAR handles the LFE channel (sub-woofer). Select from the following options in the drop-down menu:

   ❋ -12dB

   ❋ -INF—no signal from the left or right surround channel is mixed down in stereo

   ❋ Or enter a custom value

8. Mix down your project through the stereo bus.

9. Listen to your surround project as a stereo mixdown file and make adjustments to the settings if necessary.

Creating Audio for Flash

Macromedia Flash is one of the most popular applications for animation and online content creation today. Whether you're creating a band Web site or scoring an animation, it's increasingly likely that you'll be creating audio content for Flash in the future, if you're not already.

Creating Flash Audio

Unlike traditional video, Flash movies are often interactive. This may be something as simple as a main menu that loops background music while waiting for input, or it could be a full-on immersive experience where mouse gestures and clicks trigger animations and accompanying sounds.

Use the following guidelines when creating audio for Flash:

❋ To preserve the inherent flexibility of Flash, keep your audio modular. You should be able to export each theme or musical idea as a separate file.

❋ Don't get too tied into a linear progression. All of the pieces of audio should work well together in any order and not rely on a specific transition.

Creating Flash Segments

To keep file sizes small, Flash movies often rely on reusing or repeating the same segments of audio. Flash designers for whom you are providing audio will appreciate the following efforts to help them keep their options open:

❋ Don't apply fades, because they limit the capability to loop phrases in Flash. Volume effects can easily be reproduced within Flash by using ActionScript commands.

❋ If you know that a section will be looped, be sure to export it as a .wav file. Compression schemes such as MP3 can add gaps to the end of the sound. Flash can compress the looped .wav files on export, giving you small size and seamless looping.

❋ When assigning audio inside of Flash, event-based audio will often loop better than streaming audio (see Figure 8.6).

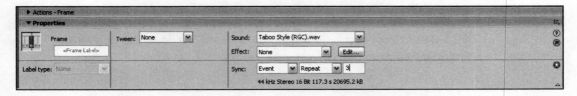

Figure 8.6

Sound properties in Flash.

Creating High-Quality Flash Audio

Hi-fidelity audio reproduction is not the main goal of Flash, so save yourself some potential headaches with the following precautions:

❋ Export 16-bit .wav files.

❋ Check your mixes in mono, because they will quite possibly end up that way (depending on the publishing options in Flash).

❋ Don't run your levels too hot. A limiter or the SONAR 5 bus preview options can ensure that you're not peaking.

❋ Consider the delivery format of the final audio. If it will be played back on laptop speakers or streamed via the Web, as is most likely, you should compress the overall mix to reduce the overall dynamic range. Also, consider that most small speakers have *no* low end and very little high end. You should audition your mix on an equivalent system.

❋ If you must use MP3s, you can export MP3s directly from SONAR to take advantage of the more flexible and higher-quality encoding (using LAME, for example). If you do this, make sure that the audio is *not* getting re-encoded in Flash. Flash has a Disable Compression option under File > Publish Settings (see Figure 8.7).

❋ If you are posting examples of your own music, you should post MP3s or WMA files separately and simply link to them through the site or Flash movie.

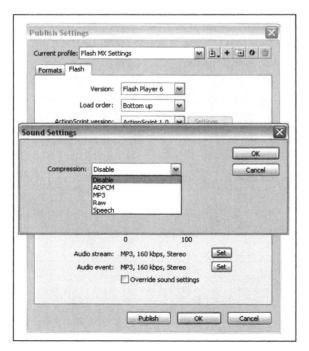

Figure 8.7

The Disable Compression setting in Flash.

Importing Flash Video

Unfortunately, SONAR cannot yet import the native Flash file format (*.SWF) directly. This reinforces the concept of keeping your music flexible and modular as detailed previously, so that you can correct any discrepancies in Flash. However, there are several methods that do allow you to work with a linear version of a Flash movie inside of SONAR.

Exporting Flash Video as an AVI File

The easiest method of getting Flash video into SONAR is to export a video directly from Flash. To do so:

1. In Flash, choose File > Export Movie.
2. In your SONAR project, choose File > Import > Video.

Exporting Flash Video as Bitmap Sequences

AVI is your best choice for general compatibility and performance. In some cases, you might find that the exported video does not play back exactly as it does in Flash. If this is the case, you can export your Flash video as a series of bitmaps (extension .bmp). Once you have created the bitmaps, you can use a program such as swf2avi to convert the series into an AVI file. To do so:

1. In Flash, choose File > Export Movie and export as a series of bitmaps.
2. Open swf2avi.
3. Choose Open and navigate to where your .bmp files are stored.
4. Add each of the .bmp files you exported in Flash (see Figure 8.8).

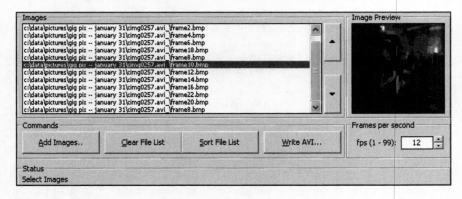

Figure 8.8
Bitmaps loaded in swf2avi, ready to be written to an AVI file.

5. Click the Write AVI button.

6. Enter a filename in the Choose a Filename to Save AVI To dialog box and click OK.

Capturing Flash Video

You can capture the movie while it is playing from a stand-alone flash player, or from within Flash itself.

In some cases, you can get accurate captures that preserve both image quality and sync. One of the most popular capture applications is Camtasia (http://www.techsmith.com/products/studio/default.asp). It features its own codec, which is optimized for screen captures.

Authoring Custom WMV Profiles

Microsoft has developed Windows Media into a space-efficient and flexible compression format for audio and video. Because Windows Media player is available on every Windows PC (and freely available for Mac), it guarantees your file a certain level of compatibility.

However, unlike some video applications, SONAR does not allow you to customize the Windows Media presets directly, instead you must select from the provided list of presets. Although this preset list is comprehensive (and confusing), there is never much of a discrepancy between the audio and video quality settings. This is rather inflexible if you want to select your audio quality apart from the video quality or if you want to set change compression and display size separately.

Fortunately, you can easily create and use new presets directly within SONAR by using the free Windows Media Profile Editor. This editor is automatically installed with the latest Windows Media Encoder, available from http://www.microsoft.com/windows/windowsmedia/9series/encoder/default.aspx.

Once you have downloaded and installed the Windows Media Profile Editor, use the following procedure to create a WMV profile:

1. Choose Start > Program Files > Windows Media > Utilities > Windows Media Profile Editor (see Figure 8.9).

2. Depending on the media type, mode, and codec used, you will be able to select a target bit-rate.

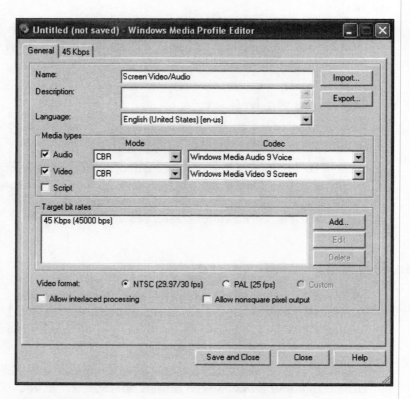

Figure 8.9

The Windows Media Profile Editor.

3. After selecting a target bit-rate, you will be able to access parameters such as display size, compression, quality, and frame rate. You might want to use the Import function to use an existing profile as a starting point. All of the profiles shipped with SONAR 5 Producer can be found in C:\Documents and Settings\All Users\Application Data\Cakewalk\ SONAR 5 Producer Edition\WMV Profiles. See Figure 8.10.

4. Either Save or Export the file to the same directory. Your new profile will now show up in the Profile drop-down list. To access this drop-down list, go to File > Export > Video, choose Windows Media Video, and then choose Encoding Options (see Figure 8.11).

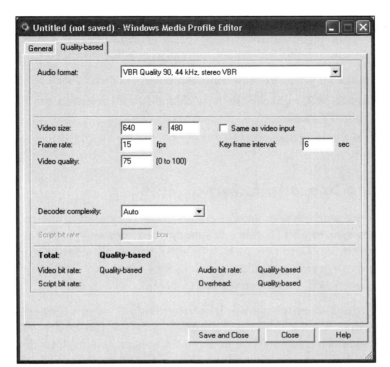

Figure 8.10
The Windows
Media Profile
Editor.

Figure 8.11
Windows Media Video
Encoding Options
dialog box.

Monitoring SONAR Video on an External Monitor

You can use a digital video (DV) player to monitor video. To do so:

1. Hook up your FireWire-compatible DV device to your computer.
2. In SONAR, right-click in the Video view and select External DV Output > *Your DV Player*.
3. Play your project.

Using SMPTE to Score to External Video

If you are working with video from an external or analog source and you need to sync to SMPTE, there are many hardware options that will allow you to convert SMPTE to MTC, which SONAR can easily slave to. For greater audio accuracy, you should use SONAR as the master and have it generate MTC (which will then be converted to SMPTE, and so on).

There are situations, however, in which you don't have access to a converter. One workaround is to "stripe" a track in SONAR, just as you would a tape. This requires a dedicated audio input and output (mono) that can record/play back the stream. Given the sound of LTC (the audio implementation of SMPTE), you will want to make sure that you have a separate trim and gain control. As with striping real tape, you obviously should bypass any processing, compression, or noise reduction on this channel.

Exporting a Section of Video

There are many situations in which it is beneficial to export a portion of a final score or dialogue, such as when you want to present updates or changes to a single section, if you want to post a finished work without the leading or trailing handles, or if you want to preview various video and audio export options before committing to a lengthy rendering cycle.

To accomplish this, you'll need to adjust the trim times in the video properties (see Figure 8.12). This is the only way to do this. Making a selection before export only affects the audio; you will still end up with a full-length video clip.

Try to only use Trim In and Trim Out before export. Afterwards, set them back. This is because SONAR uses DES (DirectShow Editing Service) whenever you change Video Properties. Using DES is much more processor-intensive than just streaming video in SONAR.

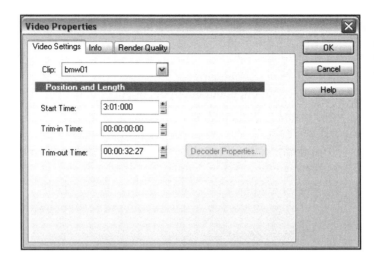

Figure 8.12

Adjusting the trim times in the Video Properties dialog box.

Setting Trim Times Using Markers

You can quickly set Trim In and Trim Out times by using markers. To do so:

1. First drop a marker where you want the video to start and stop.
2. Set each Marker to Lock to SMPTE.
3. Copy the SMPTE time displayed in the Marker dialog box (see Figure 8.13) and paste it into the Video Properties Trim In or Trim Out time.

Figure 8.13

Select and copy the SMPTE time in the Time field of the Marker dialog box.

Avoiding Audio Truncation on Video Export

You cannot lengthen video in SONAR. This means that you might find your audio truncated if it extends beyond the original length of the video. You can work around this by doing one of the following:

✳ Exporting the video and audio separately and joining them up in a video-editing application.

✳ Offsetting the start time of the video from Video Properties and then realigning the audio from within a video editor.

✳ Using a free video-editing utility such as VirtualDub (http://www.virtualdub.org/) to edit and resave the video.

Creating Surround Sound MP3s from Within SONAR

SONAR demonstrates the capabilities of surround encoding by using Windows Media and the AVI format's 5.1 support; however, you can easily expand your options using additional encoders, both free and commercial. Rather than use these encoders separately, making it a two-part process, you can access them directly from SONAR's Export dialog box. In this example, you use the new Fraunhofer MP3 Surround encoder.

1. Download and install the MP3 surround encoder (available free for non-commercial use) from http://www.iis.fraunhofer.de/amm/download/mp3surround/download-page.html. You should download the entire Demo Software file, which contains a command line encoder along with other tools.

2. To use an external encoder, you must launch the External Encoder Configuration from SONAR's Tools menu (see Figure 8.14).

3. Create a new, descriptive name, such as MP3 Surround.

4. Change the Extension to .MP3.

5. Enter any description you want, such as Fraunhofer IIS MP3 Surround encoder.

6. Set the path where the encoder is found. If you installed to the default directory, it is found at C:\Program Files\Fraunhofer IIS\MP3 Surround.

7. Enter the command line. The encoder executable is mp3sCmdlEnc.exe.

8. You must specify an input and output file by using %I and %O immediately after the executable name in the command line field.

9. Click Save.

Figure 8.14

The Cakewalk External Audio Encoder Setup dialog box.

10. From within SONAR, choose File > Export > Audio. The audio mixdown options must be 16-bit or 24-bit with a sample rate of 44.1 or 48k. The MP3 encoder works with 5.1 (6-channel) surround only and encodes CBR of 192Kbps.

Video Troubleshooting

Obviously, smooth and frame-accurate video playback is essential for proper reference. The following tips help you identify and resolve issues when playing back video from within SONAR.

Fixing Audio/Video Synchronization Issues

You might find that, although your playback seems smooth and glitch-free, sync problems develop over the course of a long video. Check the following potential problems:

❊ Confirm that the audio and video are synchronized *before* they are imported into SONAR. You could easily spend many hours troubleshooting the issue in SONAR only to find that the error occurred when the video was actually captured. Play the file in Windows Media Player from the beginning to make sure the problems are not in the file itself.

❄ Check the sample rate of the audio in the file. Here's how:

1. In Windows, right-click on the video file and select Properties.

2. Click the Summary tab (see Figure 8.15).

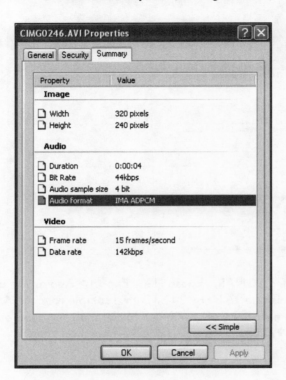

Figure 8.15
The Summary tab of the
Video Properties dialog box.

3. Click the Advanced button.

4. If this doesn't show the sample rate (it might not, depending on the format and codec), you can see the file info directly from SONAR by choosing File > Import > Video (see Figure 8.16). Before choosing File Open, note the sample rate displayed under File Info. Most video will be at 48kHz (NTSC standard is 48kHz, 16-bit), although many cameras also will capture at 32kHz. *If* there is existing audio in the project prior to importing the video and *if* the sample rate of that material is different from that of the video, SONAR will resample the audio from the video on import. Although the resampling should preserve pitch, sometimes the resampling can cause subtle shifts in timing that are noticeable during close-ups of people talking. You can confirm the sample rate of your current project before importing video by looking in File > Info > Stats. Try importing the file directly into a new file containing no audio and see if the problem occurs.

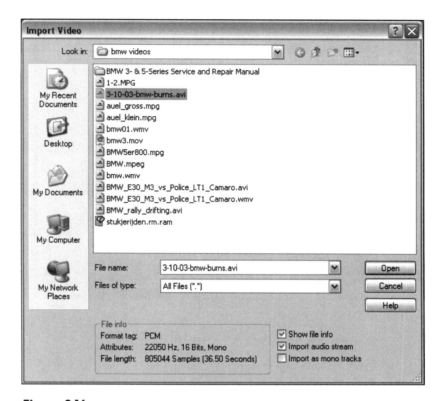

Figure 8.16

The sample rate displayed in the Import Video dialog box.

※ Check in the Aud.ini file in the SONAR 5 application directory. Open the file in a text editor such as Notepad and scroll down to the section labeled [Video]. If you see an option listed as FreewheelVideo=1, change it to FreewheelVideo=0 (see Figure 8.17). Although having this option set to 1 can improve playback consistency, it does so at the expense of timing by running video independently of the audio clock.

Figure 8.17

The line
`FreewheelVideo`
in the aud.ini file.

Fixing Inconsistent Video Playback

If the video playback is not smooth—for example if a frame freezes on screen and then jumps ahead—there might be certain settings on your computer or within the file that you can change to resolve these issues:

❋ If you have changed any of the Video Properties from within SONAR, including Trim In and Trim Out time, SONAR will use DES (DirectShow Editing Service) for playback. This immediately adds a huge performance hit, which can cause jerky playback or glitches in audio. Try changing all settings to default and removing trim and start time offsets.

❋ Check that your sound card's main output is set as the Timing Master by choosing Options > Audio > Playback Timing Master.

❋ Check your clock source by choosing Options > Project > Clock (see Figure 8.18). This should be set to internal *only* if there is no MIDI in your project and you are not using word clock synchronization from another device. In most cases, this should be audio.

❋ Check your sync settings by choosing Options > Audio > Advanced. Sync should be set to Trigger/Freewheel when syncing to SMPTE and slaving to word clock (see Figure 8.19).

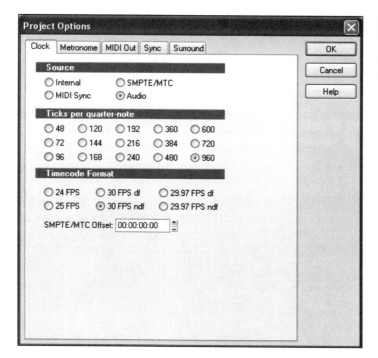

Figure 8.18

The Clock tab in the Project Options dialog box.

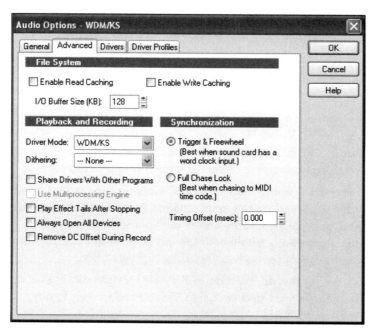

Figure 8.19

The Advanced tab in the Audio Options dialog box.

* Check your `FreewheelVideo` setting in the aud.ini file. Open the
aud.ini file from the application directory with Notepad. Under the
`[Video]` section, change or type in `FreewheelVideo=1`. This change
can cause sync issues with longer files, however, and should ideally be
used for troubleshooting purposes only.

* Check to see if any frames have dropped during playback by opening
Video Properties > Info and clicking More (see Figure 8.20). If you have
dropped frames, there may be performance issues that you need to
address.

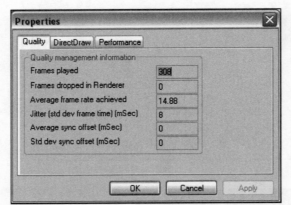

Figure 8.20

Dropped frame status in
the Properties dialog box.

Fixing Performance Issues when Playing Video

Try the following to fix video performance issues:

* As mentioned in the previous tip, avoid setting Trim or Start time offsets
from within Video Properties, because this will cause SONAR to use the
Directshow Editing Service (DES). DES leads to a performance loss,
which can adversely affect video and audio playback.

* If you are running dual (or more) monitors, see if the issue occurs when
video is played on the main monitor. Note that running different resolutions or color bit depths across multiple screens can eat up performance.
This is especially true when running at non-native resolutions or color bit
depths, because this requires software emulation.

* Try setting the video mode to Preview by right-clicking on the Video
Thumbnails view and choosing Video Properties > Render Quality
(see Figure 8.21).

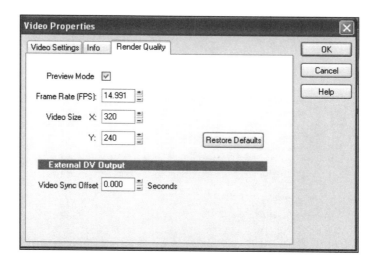

Figure 8.21

The Render Quality tab in the Video Properties dialog box.

❄ For the best performance, use an external monitor connected to the computer via FireWire. Because all of the digital-to-analog conversion of the video is done outside of the computer, it is a lot more efficient. Even if you don't have an external device like those from Pyro, you can use just about any DV camera with FireWire and component jacks as a way to connect a standard TV. Simply connect the device, power it on, and then select the device from the External DV Output list (right-click on the video or thumbnails).

❄ Of course, it is also recommended that you run the latest drivers for your display card. You should also make sure that the hardware acceleration built into your video card is being utilized. Use the following procedure to do so:

1. Choose Start > Run and type **DXDiag** (see Figure 8.22).
2. Select the Display tab and make sure that DirectDraw, Direct3D, and AGP Texture Acceleration are all set to enable. If they are not checked, you should reinstall your video card drivers or contact the manufacturer about the issue.

❄ Although compressed files take less space on a hard drive, they use more CPU cycles to decode on the fly. If you have the space, use a less compressed file, even an uncompressed AVI file. DV AVI, Indeo, and QuickTime are all good compromises between size and performance.

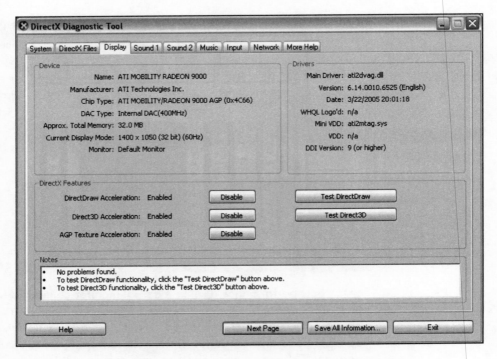

Figure 8.22

DirectX Diagnostic Tool dialog box.

Adding Keyframes for More Responsive Video Selection

If you experience issues largely when jumping between frames or looping, the problem might be with the source video itself. Most often, the video does not have enough keyframes. Having a keyframe *at least* every five frames will ensure better performance when seeking. To add more keyframes, do the following:

1. Choose Export > Video from the SONAR menu to open the Export Video dialog box.

2. Click the Encoding Options button at the bottom of the dialog box to open the AVI Encoder Options dialog box (see Figure 8.23).

3. Select a codec you want to use to export the video. You must select one other than the default in order to adjust the keyframe rate.

4. Change the keyframe rate to a number between 1 and 5.

5. Click OK to close the dialog box and Save to export the video.

6. Re-import the video into your project.

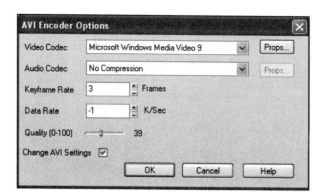

Figure 8.23

AVI Encoder Options dialog box.

Identifying and Correcting Codec Problems

Assuming you are using a format that SONAR supports (AVI, MPEG, WMV, and MOV), the most common cause of import issues involves codecs. This is especially true when trying to import content created on other machines, where the installed codecs can vary wildly from what is installed on your machine. If the issue is codec-related, you will have issues with playing it in Windows Media Player as well.

Gspot Codec Information Appliance is a free application available from http://www.headbands.com/gspot/. Gspot will analyze any video file you drag into it. It will then tell you what codec is used, if you have the codec installed or not, and it can even attempt to play the file. This latter function is useful for identifying other issues with files that fail to load or play back as well. Figure 8.24 shows Gspot loaded with .bmp files, ready to convert the series into an AVI file.

Once you have identified the codec, you will hopefully be able to obtain it via a Web site or third-party application install. If not, you will have to re-export the file from the original computer and select a different codec. The View > Codecs option in Gspot allows you to see which codecs are installed on your machine so you can select a compatible codec for use on any imported video.

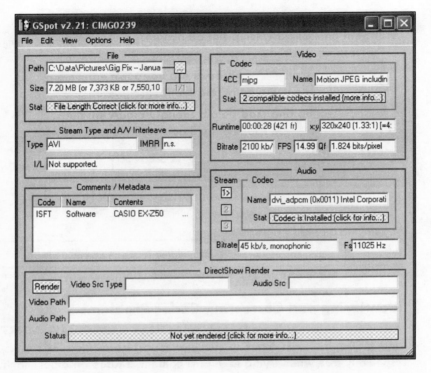

Figure 8.24

Gspot Codec Information Appliance.

Several free popular codecs include:

❀ DivX—http://www.divx.com/divx/

❀ XviD—http://www.xvid.org/

❀ Techsmith Capture Codec—http://www.techsmith.com/download/
    codecsdefault.asp?lid=CodecsHome

Export problems are most often caused by trying to pass an incompatible audio or video format to the encoder. This also includes using an incompatible sample rate or bit depth. Most encoders accept 16-bit at 44.1 or 48kHz, so try this format when in doubt.

There can also be an issue with the codec you are using. Reinstall the codec or select a different one.

Preserving Multi-Track Audio when Transferring Between Video Applications

When working with video, SONAR might not be the last stop. To preserve flexibility when transferring video and its associated audio in and out of SONAR, it is helpful to preserve separation among voiceover tracks, music, and sound and Foley effects.

In addition to using OMF (detailed in Chapter 7), there are two other options for exporting uncompressed, multi-channel audio files. In either scenario, you must set up SONAR as if you are working with surround. Send each mono or stereo track to a surround bus. Make sure that each track is hard-panned to a specific channel (L, R, C, RS, or LS). You can ensure this by muting other channels in the Surround Panner.

To export multi-channel audio only:

1. Choose File > Export Audio (see Figure 8.25).

Figure 8.25

The Export Audio dialog box.

2. Choose RIFF Wav.

3. Set Source Category to Busses, Main Outputs, or Entire Mix.

4. Set Channel Format to Multi-channel.

5. Export.

To export multi-channel audio and video:

1. Choose File > Export Video.

2. Choose Video for Windows.

3. Select Audio Mixdown Options and ensure that Multi-channel is selected in the Channel Format menu.

4. Click OK to close the Audio Mixdown Options dialog box.

5. Click the Save button in the Video Export dialog to export.

A Keyboard Shortcuts

Table A.1 Menu Commands

Command	Shortcut
File-Open	Ctrl-O
File-Save	Ctrl-S
Edit-Undo	Ctrl-Z
Edit-Redo	Ctrl-Shift-Z
Edit-Select-All	Ctrl-A
Edit-Select-None	Ctrl-Shift-A
Edit-Cut	Ctrl-X
Edit-Copy	Ctrl-C
Edit-Paste	Ctrl-V
Edit-Delete	Delete key
Insert-Marker	F11
Transport-Play	Spacebar
Transport-Record	R
Transport-Rewind	W
Transport-Stop	Spacebar
Transport-Tempo Ratio 1	Ctrl-1
Transport-Tempo Ratio 2	Ctrl-2
Transport-Tempo Ratio 3	Ctrl-3

(continues)

Table A.1 Menu Commands *(continued)*

Command	Shortcut
Go-Time	F5
Go-From	F7
Go-Thru	F8
Go-Beginning	Ctrl+Home
Go-End	Ctrl+End
Go-Previous Measure	Ctrl+PageUp
Go-Next Measure	Ctrl+PageDown
Go-Previous Marker	Ctrl+Shift+PageUp
Go-Next Marker	Ctrl+Shift+PageDn
Go-Search Next	F3
Tools-Run CAL	Ctrl+F1

Table A.2 Track View

Command	Shortcut
Solo/un-solo current track	/
Help	F1
Close Window	Ctrl+F4
Insert track	Insert
Open the Track Manager	M
Show/hide Bus pane	Shift+B
Toggle Envelope/Offset Mode	O
Select current track	, (comma key)
Show and fit selection	Shift+S
Fit tracks to window	F
Fit project to window	Shift+F
Show only selected tracks	H
Hide selected tracks	Shift+H
Show all tracks	A
Undo view change	U

Command	Shortcut
Redo view change	Shift-U
Snap enable/disable	N
Open Snap dialog	Shift-N
Activate Zoom tool	Z
Decrease track height	Ctrl-up arrow
Increase track height	Ctrl-down arrow
Zoom in horizontally	Ctrl-right arrow
Zoom out horizontally	Ctrl-left arrow
Zoom all tracks in vertically	Ctrl-down arrow
Zoom all tracks out vertically	Ctrl-up arrow
Zoom out on all audio waveforms	Alt-down arrow
Zoom in on current track's audio waveforms	Alt-Ctrl-up arrow
Zoom out on current track's audio waveforms	Alt-Ctrl-down arrow
Zoom current track in vertically	Ctrl-Shift-down arrow
Zoom current track out vertically	Ctrl-Shift-up arrow
Zoom in on all audio waveforms	Alt-up arrow
Increase current track height	Ctrl-Shift-down arrow
Decrease current track height	Ctrl-Shift-up arrow
Scale audio waveform in all audio tracks	Alt-up/down arrow
Scale audio waveform in current audio track	Ctrl-Alt-up/down arrow
Lasso zoom scale audio clip/waveform	Shift-Z (while selecting a clip)
Scissors tool	C
Center Now time	G
Puts focus in Track pane	Shift-Up arrow
Puts focus in Bus pane	Shift-Down arrow
Scroll Track view up or down	Page Up or Page Down
Move between same controls in different tracks	Up or Down arrow
Move between controls in same track	Left or Right arrow
Moves to the previous or next tab in Track pane (All, Mix, FX, I/O)	Shift-Left arrow or Shift-Right arrow
Raise or lower the pitch of a loop-enabled clip	Alt+ or Alt- (use the + or - keys on the num pad)
Activate Select tool	T

(continues)

Table A.2 Track View *(continued)*

Command	Shortcut
Activate Scrub tool	B
Activate Envelope Edit tool	E
Loop enable/disable selected clip	Ctrl+L
Split selected clips at Now time	S
Auto crossfade	X
Toggle on/off "sticky" Now Time (Now Time returns to Now Time Marker on stop)	Ctrl+Spacebar
Toggle display of the Track Inspector	I
Open/close current track folder	Ctrl+F
Mute tool on/off	K
Mute or unmute selected clips	Q
Show/hide Navigator pane	D
Show/hide Video Thumbnail pane	L
Nudge left 1	NumPad 1
Nudge right 1	NumPad 3
Nudge left 2	NumPad 4
Nudge right 2	NumPad 6
Nudge left 3	NumPad 7
Nudge right 3	NumPad 9
Nudge up	NumPad 8
Nudge down	NumPad 2

Table A.3 Piano Roll View

Command	Shortcut
Select tool	S
Draw tool	D **Note**: you can draw straight lines with the Draw tool by holding the Shift key down before and while you draw.
Pattern Brush Tool	Q
Scrub tool	B
Enter a Whole Note	1
Enter a Half Note	2
Enter a Quarter Note	4
Enter an Eighth Note	8
Enter a Sixteenth Note	6
Enter a Thirty-second Note	3
Dotted Note	. (period key)
Triplet	P
Snap enable/disable	N
Open Snap dialog	Shift·N
Pick Track	T
Show/Hide Track Pane	H
Show/Hide the Controller pane	C
All Tracks	A
No Tracks	K
Invert Tracks	V
Show/Hide velocity tails in the Drum pane	Y
Show/Hide Grid lines	I
Show/Hide durations in the Drum pane	O
Zoom tool	Z
Scroll up/down	Up or Down arrow keys
Scroll left/right	Left or Right arrow keys
Zoom in vertically	Ctrl·down arrow
Zoom out vertically	Ctrl·up arrow
Undo Zoom	U

Table A.4 Staff View

Command	Shortcut
Select tool	S
Draw tool	D
Erase tool	E
Scrub tool	B
Lyric	Y
Chord	C
Expression	I
Hairpin	H
Pedal	A
Snap enable/disable	N
Fill Durations	F
Trim Durations	M
Layout	L
Pick Track	T
Whole note	1
Half note	2
Quarter note	4
Eighth note	8
Sixteenth note	6
Thirty-second note	3
Dotted	. (period key)
Triplet	P
Scroll left/right	arrow keys
Play Previous Note	Ctrl+left arrow
Play Next Note	Ctrl+right arrow
Open Snap dialog	Shift+N
Export to ASCII TAB	X
Show/Hide Fretboard view	V

Table A.5 Event List View

Command	Shortcut
Filter (hide) Note events	N
Filter Key Aftertouch events	F
Filter Controller events	C
Filter Patch Change events	A
Filter Channel Aftertouch Events	F
Filter Pitch Wheel events	B
Filter RPN events	Z
Filter NRPN events	P
Filter Sysx Bank events	S
Filter Sysx Data events	Y
Filter Text events	X
Filter Lyric events	L
Filter MCI Command events	M
Filter Audio events	U
Filter Shape events	H
Filter Expression events	E
Filter Hairpin events	I
Filter Chord events	O
Event Manager	V
Insert event	Insert
Delete event	Delete
Play single event	Ctrl+Shift+Spacebar
Pick Tracks	T

Table A.6 Console View

Command	Shortcut
Move between controls	Tab
Delete an effect	Delete
Change values (small)	+ and -
Change values (large)	[and]
Open Module manager	M
Toggle Envelope/Offset Mode	O

Table A.7 Loop Construction View

Command	Shortcut
Save loop to wave file	F
Enable looping	L
Enable stretching	T
Follow project pitch	P
Preview loop	Ctrl+Shift+Spacebar
Stop preview	Ctrl+Shift+Spacebar
Select tool	S
Erase marker tool	E
Default all markers	M
Enable Slice Auto-Preview	A
Slice Auto-Preview Loop	Shift+A
Clip Properties	C
Move to Previous Slice	PageUp
Move to Next Slice	PageDown
Show/Hide Gain Envelope	G
Show/Hide Pan Envelope	N
Show/Hide Pitch Envelope	K

Table A.8 Synth Rack View

Command	Shortcut
Navigate between synths	Up/Down arrows
Change preset for current soft synth	+ or -
Insert	A
Delete	D
Properties	P
Open Insert Soft Synth Options dialog	O
Freeze	Shift+F
Unfreeze	Shift+U
Quick Unfreeze	Shift+T
Mute current soft synth	M
Solo current soft synth	S

Table A.9 All Views

Command	Shortcut
Close Window	Ctrl+F4
Next Window	Ctrl+F6
Open the Loop Explorer view	Alt+1
Open the Loop Construction view	Alt+2
Open the Console view	Alt+3
Open the Event List view	Alt+4
Open the Piano Roll view	Alt+5
Open the Video view	Alt+6
Open the Staff view	Alt+7
Open the Lyrics view	Alt+8
Open the Tempo view	Alt+9

Table A.10 Loop Explorer View

Command	Shortcut
Preview file	Ctrl·Shift·Spacebar
Stop preview	Ctrl·Shift·Spacebar

Table A.11 Surround Panner (large)

Command	Shortcut
Constrains to angle	Alt·drag
Constrains to angle at 100% focus	Alt·Shift·drag
Constrains to focus only	Ctrl·Shift·drag
Sets panner point to the point that you click	Shift·click
Fine resolution	Shift·drag controls (Angle, Width, etc.)
Move to next/previous widget in surround panner	Up/Down cursor keys
Move to next/previous panner in same track	Left/Right cursor keys
Move to surround panner in another track	Ctrl·up/down
Speaker mutes	Ctrl·NumPad 0–9
Jump to speaker angle at 100% focus	NumPad 1–9
Ls	NumPad 1
Cs	NumPad 2
Rs	NumPad 3
Sl	NumPad 4
Sr	NumPad 6
L	NumPad 7
C	NumPad 8
R	NumPad 9
Lc	/
Rc	*

# Index

plug-ins, restoring corrupted projects, 22
preamps, overdriving effects, 36
pre-faders, track muting, 111–112
Pro Tools
    filename size limit work-around, 195–197
    importing key bindings, 16
    OMF (Open Media Format) file support, 189
Processor Scheduling, ASIO drivers, 4–5
processors
    ASIO driver scheduling, 4–5
    cycle conservation, 176–177
    external processor latency compensation, 156–158
    external processors access methods, 100–103
    Freeze command conservation techniques, 88–89
    stand-alone CPU, 92–93
Project Options dialog box
    audio metronome bus settings, 35
    clock settings, 240–241
    custom metronome sounds, 53–54
    downmixing, 226–227
    multiple computer synchronization, 93–94
    Zero All Controllers on Stop, 18
projects
    backup strategies, 12–13
    CD mastering, 207–214
    collaboration methods, 188–189
    restoring corrupted, 22–23
    track sorts, 21
Properties dialog box, dropped frame status display, 242
PRV Mode, Track view, 131

Q

Quantize command, phrase/beat alignments, 83
Quantize tool, rhythm track editing, 74–77
quick grouping, mixing controls, 122
Quick Unfreeze command, sample-based synths, 89

R

rackmount PCs, live show recording, 49–50
radio, cheap radio effects, 168–169

RAID (Redundant Array of Inexpensive Disks) arrays
    configuration, 3
    hard drive coolers, 12
RAM, page file configuration, 8–9
README files, OMF (Open Media Format) file inclusion, 190, 192
Reassign Control command, automating effects, 172–173
recording
    ADAT lightpipes, 45–47
    custom metronome sounds, 53–54
    hard disk recorders, 48
    keyboard as remote control, 44–45
    live shows, 48–50
    MIDI foot control, 42–44
    MIDI w/o armed track, 52
    non-destructive external effects, 42
    one-hand step, 25–27
    vocal track looping, 62–64
redundancy, RAID arrays, 3
Redundant Array of Inexpensive Disks (RAID) arrays, configuration, 3
Regenerate Tablature dialog box, guitar TAB transcription, 133–134
Registry
    importing/exporting color presets, 201–202
    importing/exporting custom scales, 199–200
    importing/exporting effects presets, 197–199
    Windows XP performance enhancements, 6–7
remixing
    Nudge command techniques, 59
    vocals, 82–85
Remote Control dialog box
    automating effects, 172–173
    remapping MIDI controllers, 184–185
remote controls
    keyboard as, 44–45
    MIDI foot control, 42–44
removable media, backup strategies, 12–13
Remove Silence command
    breath noise removal, 77
    Cakewalk Bundle file size reduction, 192–193
    rhythm track editing, 75–76